THE CAMBRIDGE BIBLE COMMENTARY

NEW ENGLISH BIBLE

GENERAL EDITORS
P. R. ACKROYD, A. R. C. LEANEY, J. W. PACKER

THE LETTERS OF PETER AND JUDE

THE CAMBRIDGE BIBLE COMMENTARY

The Gospel according to Matthew A. W. Argyle
The Gospel according to Mark C. F. D. Moule
The Gospel according to Luke E. J. Tinsley
The Gospel according to John A. M. Hunter
Acts of the Apostles J. W. Packer
The Letter of Paul to the Romans Ernest Best
The Letters of Paul to the Corinthians Margaret Thrall
The Letter of Paul to the Galatians W. Neil
The Letters of Paul to the Ephesians, the Colossians and to Philemon
  G. H. D. Thompson
The Letters of Paul to the Philippians and the Thessalonians K. Grayson
The Pastoral Letters A. T. Hanson
A Letter to Hebrews J. H. Davies
The Letters of John and James R. R. Williams
The Letters of Peter and Jude A. R. C. Leaney
The Revelation of John T. F. Glasson
Understanding the New Testament edited by O. Jessie Lace
New Testament Illustrations Maps, diagrams, and photographs collected and
  introduced by Clifford M. Jones

THE LETTERS OF
PETER AND JUDE

A COMMENTARY ON THE FIRST LETTER OF PETER,
A LETTER OF JUDE AND THE
SECOND LETTER OF PETER

A. R. C. LEANEY

Reader in Theology at the University of Nottingham

CAMBRIDGE
AT THE UNIVERSITY PRESS
1967

Published by the Syndics of the Cambridge University Press
Bentley House, 200 Euston Road, London, N.W. 1
American Branch: 32 East 57th Street, New York, N.Y. 10022

Library of Congress Catalogue Card Number: 66–29214

Printed in Great Britain
at the University Printing House, Cambridge
(Brooke Crutchley, University Printer)

GENERAL EDITORS' PREFACE

The aim of this series is to provide the text of the New English Bible closely linked to a commentary in which the results of modern scholarship are made available to the general reader. Teachers and young people preparing for such examinations as the General Certificate of Education at Ordinary or Advanced Level in Britain and similar qualifications elsewhere have been especially kept in mind. The commentators have been asked to assume no specialized theological knowledge, and no knowledge of Greek and Hebrew. Bare references to other literature and multiple references to other parts of the Bible have been avoided. Actual quotations have been given as often as possible.

Within these quite severe limits each commentator will attempt to set out the main findings of recent New Testament scholarship, and to describe the historical background to the text. The main theological content of the New Testament will also be critically discussed.

Much attention has been given to the form of the volumes. The aim is to produce books each of which will be read consecutively from first to last page. The introductory material leads naturally into the text, which itself leads into the alternating sections of commentary.

The series is prefaced by a volume—*Understanding the New Testament*—which outlines the larger historical background, says something about the growth and transmission of the text, and answers the question 'Why should we study the New Testament?' Another volume—*New Testament Illustrations*—contains maps, diagrams and photographs.   P.R.A.   A.R.C.L.   J.W.P.

CONTENTS

THE FIRST LETTER OF PETER

✻ ✻ ✻ ✻ ✻ ✻ ✻ ✻ ✻ ✻ ✻ ✻ ✻

Peter, apostle of Jesus Christ   *page* 3

God's scattered people   6

The writer   7

✻ ✻ ✻ ✻ ✻ ✻ ✻ ✻ ✻ ✻ ✻ ✻ ✻

The Calling of a Christian   13

✻ ✻ ✻ ✻ ✻ ✻ ✻ ✻ ✻ ✻ ✻ ✻ ✻

A LETTER OF JUDE
THE SECOND LETTER OF PETER

✻ ✻ ✻ ✻ ✻ ✻ ✻ ✻ ✻ ✻ ✻ ✻ ✻

Structure   77

✻ ✻ ✻ ✻ ✻ ✻ ✻ ✻ ✻ ✻ ✻ ✻ ✻

Jude, servant of Jesus Christ   81

The Danger of False Belief (Jude)   82

✻ ✻ ✻ ✻ ✻ ✻ ✻ ✻ ✻ ✻ ✻ ✻ ✻

The author   100

Parallels between Jude and 2 Peter   101

The Remedy for Doubt (2 Peter)   105

✻ ✻ ✻ ✻ ✻ ✻ ✻ ✻ ✻ ✻ ✻ ✻ ✻

The Christian hope   140

✻ ✻ ✻ ✻ ✻ ✻ ✻ ✻ ✻ ✻ ✻ ✻ ✻

INDEX   144

THE FIRST LETTER OF PETER

THE FIRST LETTER OF
PETER

✳ ✳ ✳ ✳ ✳ ✳ ✳ ✳ ✳ ✳ ✳ ✳ ✳

'Peter, apostle of Jesus Christ' (1 Pet. 1: 1)

Simon Peter, also known as Cephas, the spokesman of the disciples in the gospels, is the chief of the twelve apostles in the early chapters of Acts. There he takes the lead in the election of Matthias into Judas's place (1: 15), addresses the crowd after the coming of the Holy Spirit on the day of Pentecost (2: 1–40), heals a lame man at the 'Beautiful Gate' (3: 1–10), and speaks forcefully to the crowd which gathers round (3: 12–26). He and John (son of Zebedee) are twice brought before the Sanhedrin for healing and preaching in Jesus's name (4: 7–22 and 5: 18, 27–42), on the second of these two occasions being set free on the advice of Gamaliel (5: 33–9). When the church moves outwards, the Holy Spirit persuades Peter by a dream at Joppa and by his experience at Caesarea in the house of the centurion Cornelius that 'God has no favourites, but that in every nation the man who is godfearing and does what is right is acceptable to him' (10: 34 f.). Peter defends this visit to Cornelius when he returns to Jerusalem (11: 1–18). At some time between A.D. 41 and 44 King Herod (Agrippa I) 'beheaded James...' and 'proceeded to arrest Peter' (Acts 12: 2 f.) but Peter was miraculously delivered from prison (12: 6–17). We do not know the exact date; Agrippa's death is recorded in the same chapter and we know this happened in A.D. 44, but we do not know how long after Peter's escape Herod Agrippa died. It was after he had resided 'for a time at Caesarea' (12: 20). This is vague, and there are difficulties about understanding

3

Peter's movements. When he left Jerusalem (12: 17) he was a fugitive from prison. It is hard to see how he could be back in the city without any explanation, as in Acts 15. Perhaps his journeys, recorded in Acts 9: 32 ('a general tour'), to Lydda, Joppa and Caesarea, when he met Cornelius, really took place *after* he left Jerusalem; and perhaps this was when 'Cephas' (i.e. Peter) 'came to Antioch' (Gal. 2: 11) and was rebuked there by Paul for going back on the liberal position towards the Gentiles which he had so recently learnt was the teaching of the Holy Spirit. He seems at first to have believed that 'God has no favourites' (Acts 10: 34), for 'until certain persons came from James he was taking his meals with gentile Christians; but when they came he drew back and began to hold aloof' (Gal. 2: 12), so he seems not quite to have had the courage of his own convictions. If we study the problems raised by the Acts of the Apostles we find that it is not easy to decide when the council related in Acts 15 took place, and especially how and when James became the head of the church at Jerusalem. If the council is out of its proper place in the story, or if Peter was not really present at it, we can imagine that he left Jerusalem after escaping from prison and never returned. This would be how he came to visit not only Lydda, Joppa, Caesarea and Antioch, but also perhaps Corinth; for there was a group at Corinth who said, referring to him by the other form of his name, 'I follow Cephas' (1 Cor. 1: 12), and Paul speaks of him as travelling with his Christian wife (1 Cor. 9: 5).

We do not know the name of Peter's wife or anything about her except that Jesus healed her mother (Mark 1: 29–31 and parallels). Her story is one of many which it would be most interesting to have, but the ancient world often did not think women important enough to mention, and Luke says nothing about her in Acts.

She may well have been with Peter in Rome, even though she is not mentioned, for that seems to be where Peter was at the end of his life. It is not she but the Church in 'Babylon' (i.e. Rome) which is meant in I Peter 5: 13. We shall see that perhaps we ought not to rely on 1 Pet. 5: 13 as evidence for this, and there is no other evidence in the New Testament that Peter did go to Rome, but we must respect the strong tradition that he did, though its historical foundations are now no longer easy to produce. Clement of Rome, writing his letter to the Corinthians, perhaps about A.D. 96, refers to Peter in a way which many think implies that the apostle had met his death by martyrdom at Rome, but it is not at all clear that Clement means at Rome, since he does not mention any place at all (1 Clem. 5: 1–4). The church historian Eusebius (*c.* 260–340) preserves for us some interesting traditions about Peter and Paul in Rome: he tells us that Dionysius, bishop of Corinth, writing to the Romans (in about A.D. 170), speaks of 'the planting that came from Peter and Paul'. Planting means founding churches, presumably; but neither Peter nor Paul actually founded the church at Rome. Little is known of its foundation, but it took place early enough for Paul to write his famous letter to the Romans in about A.D. 55. Dionysius says again, '...and likewise they taught together also in Italy and were martyred on the same occasion.' Further, a presbyter of the church at Rome named Caius said he could 'point out the trophies' (memorials) 'of the apostles'. In the passage quoted above, Eusebius also relates the tradition that both apostles were put to death under Nero (*Ecclesiastical History*, 2. 25. 5 ff.). This would be in the barbaric act of cruelty, confined to Rome itself, by which Nero, to get rid of the report that Rome had been fired by his orders, 'fastened the guilt...on a class hated for their abominations, called Christians by the populace', as Tacitus wrote in his *Annals*, 15: 44. This was in A.D. 64, so if the First Letter really was written by Peter it cannot have been later than that year. But we shall see (pp. 7 ff.) that there are good reasons for holding that the letter was not written by Peter, but in his name by some person who felt it an honour to write on behalf of the church where he was regarded as a founding apostle.

*'God's scattered people who lodge for a while in Pontus,
Galatia, Cappadocia, Asia, and Bithynia'* (1 Pet. 1: 1)

Pontus and *Bithynia* had been united as one province of the
Roman Empire since 64 B.C., but there is no evidence of a
Christian church there until the governorship of Pliny the
Younger in *c.* A.D. 112. This evidence implies that Christianity
had been there for at least twenty years, but not so early that
a letter could have been written to an established church there
in or before A.D. 64 (the presumed date of Peter's death).
Galatia, a province including, since 25 B.C., Pisidia, Lycaonia
and Isauria, had been evangelized by Paul (Acts 13–14 and the
Letter to the Galatians). So had *Asia* (the province in the west
of the area usually called Asia Minor, which includes all

6

those places mentioned here along with Mysia, Lydia and Caria). Ephesus was the capital of Asia (Acts 19, etc.). *Cappadocia*, a province since A.D. 17, is mentioned elsewhere in the New Testament only at Acts 2:9; as one of the places whence those present in Jersualem at Pentecost had come. It lay immediately north of Cilicia and may have been evangelized from there fairly early, although we have no evidence for this other than the mention here. The districts are all among those which we know Paul to have evangelized or which we may reasonably assume to have received the gospel indirectly through him.

The Writer

Peter may have visited the districts listed in verse 1 because it was agreed, as Paul tells us in Gal. 2:7, that he 'had been entrusted with the Gospel for Jews' and he may have taken the gospel to Jews in these areas; but we have absolutely no other evidence for his having gone there.

When the letter was written, a persecution was evidently in progress against the Christians to whom the letter is addressed. 4:12 ff. ('the fiery ordeal that is upon you') makes this certain. If Peter wrote it, the persecution in question must be that of A.D. 64, which was confined to Rome. Perhaps Peter wrote to warn his old converts far away of the possibility that it would reach them, and to teach them how to face it; though he might be too preoccupied with the situation in Rome to do even that. Eusebius accepts the First Letter of Peter 'as authentic and accepted by the early Fathers' (*Eccl. Hist.* 3.3).

There are reasons for doubting whether the letter was literally *from Peter*. The good Greek in which it is written and the quotations from the Septuagint (the Greek version of the Old Testament) do not suggest the Galilaean fisherman, who was far from illiterate, but is no doubt fairly described in Acts 4:13 as an 'untrained layman'. It has been argued that the style and some of the thought of the letter are due to the

Silvanus mentioned at 5: 12, and that he is to be identified with the Silas who was Paul's companion (Acts 15: 27 onwards) and part author of the letters to the Thessalonians (1 Thess. 1: 1 and 2 Thess. 1: 1). This would be a good argument if we wanted to hold that 1 Peter is a letter of Silvanus; but the more we say that Silvanus's help is the explanation of things which make us doubt that Peter wrote it, the less likely we make it that Peter did write it.

The letter is addressed to people being persecuted; but there is no indication that the writer is (which would be the situation if Peter wrote it). What then was the situation? Let us consider some of the interesting evidence provided by the letter itself. We shall see that perhaps not all of it is—or was originally—a letter. The first clue is that the work makes a stop at 4: 11 with a doxology, an ascription to God of glory and power, like the formal end of a sermon in church. As far as this point, the work is not particularly like a letter, since it does not take up different subjects or answer questions, nor does it betray any controversy or discussion with the readers. It is, on the other hand, an attractive and persuasive discourse, based on the idea that those being exhorted have all been baptized; reminding them of this gives the writer the opportunity to remind them also of their Christian profession. After this point, on the other hand, the work becomes very like a letter, since it refers clearly to an event now in progress, 'the fiery ordeal that is upon you' (4: 12). It is therefore possible that a letter has been added to a work originally much more like a sermon given in church; and the rest of the last part certainly looks much more like an actual letter.

It seems therefore that some person or persons may have sent a discourse—perhaps a favourite sermon—to their Christian brethren on hearing that they were in danger of persecution. These people must have been living in Pontus, Galatia, Cappodocia, Asia and Bithynia. Then 1: 1–2 and 4: 12 — 5: 14 make a 'letter framework' for the main part, which is a sermon enclosed in the letter. By an interesting chance we know of a situation which this would fit very well: in about A.D. 112 Pliny the governor of Bithynia-Pontus wrote to the emperor Trajan for guidance on a difficult question. The letter is numbered Pliny, *Epp.* 10: 96, and in it Pliny writes as follows:

> In investigations of Christians I have never taken part; hence I do not know what is the crime usually punished or investigated...whether punishment attaches to the mere name apart from secret crimes, or to the secret crimes connected with the name. Meantime this is the course I have taken...I asked them whether they were Christians, and if they confessed, I asked them a second and third time with threats of punishment. If they kept to it, I ordered them for execution...those who said that they neither were nor ever had been Christians, I thought it right to let go, since they recited a prayer to the gods at my dictation, made supplication with incense and wine to your statue...and moreover cursed Christ—things which... those who are really Christians cannot be made to do. Others said that they were Christians and then denied it, explaining that they had been, but had ceased to be such, some three years ago, some a good many years, and a few twenty. They maintained that the amount of their fault or error had been this, that it was their habit on a fixed day to assemble before daylight and recite by turns a form of words to Christ as a god; and that they bound themselves with an oath, not for any crime, but not to commit theft or robbery or adultery, not to break their word, and not to deny a deposit when demanded. After this was done, their custom was to depart, and to meet again to take food, but ordinary and harmless food.

Although Pliny asks whether it is a crime merely to be a Christian—'whether punishment attaches to the mere name' —he makes clear that he did in fact punish people who confessed to being Christians and nothing more wicked than that, and in his reply Trajan said he had done the right thing. With this we can compare 1 Pet. 4: 16, addressed to people some of whom at least were in the same province as Pliny's in A.D. 112: '...if anyone suffers as a Christian, he should feel it no disgrace, but confess that name to the honour of God.' A further point is worth making: Pliny speaks of Christians who had renounced their faith as long as twenty years before. He does not say that they recanted under persecution, but it is possible that they did so, and the date would then be roughly the time when Domitian cruelly treated those who refused to worship the emperor, that is, about A.D. 96. It is a widely accepted view that the book of Revelation belongs to that time, its author John being exiled to the island of Patmos for his loyalty to Jesus (in Rev. 1: 9 he says, 'I was on the island called Patmos because I had preached God's word and borne my testimony to Jesus'). In the book of Revelation, Rome is called Babylon (14: 8; 16: 19; 17: 5; and three times in chapter 18); and this is a new departure, for Rome is not in the earlier books of the New Testament regarded as the arch-enemy, if an enemy at all. In Acts, Roman governors sometimes help Paul. Thus, calling Rome by the name Babylon, the great oppressor city of Old Testament times, in 1 Pet. 5: 13, suggests that the work was written relatively late, and it becomes all the more reasonable to suppose that it fits in with the situation found in Bithynia in the time of Pliny.

If this is right, Peter cannot have written the letter, and an important question remains unanswered: why did the writers or writer send their letter or sermon in the name of Peter? The only guess we can make is that Peter was at this time associated with Rome, and that by writing in Peter's name the author meant to suggest that he was writing on behalf of the church there. This is far from impossible, for Eusebius believes that Peter's association with Rome is historical, and dates from about A.D. 60. The evidence for Peter *being believed* to have been in Rome and to have taught there is quite firm

when we come to a date early in the second century. Eusebius
in his first book refers to the tradition in Clement of Alexandria's *Outlines* (towards the end of the second century)
that the Gospel according to Mark was written as a result of
people who had heard Peter preach in Rome begging Mark
to write a summary of this teaching for them. More important,
Eusebius says this is confirmed by Papias (A.D. *c.* 60–130), bishop
of Hierapolis (a city of Asia Minor near Colossae—see Col.
4: 13), 'who also points out that Mark is mentioned by Peter
in his first epistle, which he is said to have composed in Rome
itself, as he himself indicates when he speaks of the city
figuratively as Babylon: "Greetings from her who dwells in
Babylon, chosen by God like you, and from my son Mark,"'
(*Eccl. Hist.* 2: 15). In Book Three of his History Eusebius
refers to Papias again on the subject of the association of
Mark with Peter, and quotes Papias as saying that his inform-
ant 'the presbyter' used to say: 'Mark, who had been Peter's
interpreter, wrote carefully, but not in order, all that he
remembered of the Lord's sayings and doings...' (*Eccl.
Hist.* 3: 39). There are difficulties about believing that this
was really the origin of Mark's gospel, but Papias's words are
evidence for people in Asia Minor believing at least as early as
A.D. 130 that Peter had been in Rome with Mark. Had this
been caused or fostered by the words of 1 Pet. 5: 13? See
the commentary on 5: 13 for the possible ways of interpreting
'my son Mark', and on 5: 12 for the possible identity of
Silvanus if we reject the idea that he was the Silas of Paul's
journey into Europe and part author of the letters to the
Thessalonians.

Modern readers are sometimes shocked at the suggestion
that a writer would write under the name of a famous man
and give no clue to his own identity. This is because they do
not understand the custom of the ancient world in this matter.
A very large number of books which were written by earnest
religious people to warn, encourage and strengthen their
readers, especially in the times between the Old and New

Testaments, are written as though by very famous men of the past. Such are the books of Enoch and the Testaments of the Twelve Patriarchs; no one would think of suggesting that these were really written by the Enoch of Gen. 5: 24 or by the actual patriarchs. The convention by which these works were written as though by these famous personages was certainly shared by the Christian church, and accounts for a spate of writing after New Testament times, when a large number of books appeared under the names of apostles although no one believed apostles had really written them. There is little doubt that this convention accounts for a number of writings in the New Testament itself. Eusebius, as we saw, accepts the First Letter of Peter; the remarkable thing is that he does not accept the second, although it is that letter which seems to contain the testimony of an eyewitness of events in the Gospel. For in 2 Pet. 1: 16 f. the author refers to the Transfiguration (described in Mark 9: 2–8 and parallel passages in Luke and Matthew) and then adds in verse 18, 'This voice from heaven we ourselves heard; when it came, we were with him on the sacred mountain.' 2 Pet. 3: 1 remarks, 'This is now my second letter to you, my friends'. Such an author would not mean by this to deceive the readers into thinking he was really Peter the apostle; whether he himself thought Peter was the author of the First Letter or not, his words here only illustrate how innocent it was considered to take the name of a famous man when writing a religious work.

If we give due weight to all these considerations we may well come to the conclusions that 2 Peter is certainly pseudo-nymous (written under an assumed name) and that 1 Peter may be so, although the early church accepted it as authentic.

✳   ✳   ✳   ✳   ✳   ✳   ✳   ✳   ✳   ✳   ✳   ✳   ✳

The Calling of a Christian

OPENING GREETINGS

FROM PETER, apostle of Jesus Christ, to those of God's **1**
scattered people who lodge for a while in Pontus,
Galatia, Cappadocia, Asia, and Bithynia—chosen of old **2**
in the purpose of God the Father, hallowed to his service
by the Spirit, and consecrated with the sprinkled blood of
Jesus Christ.

Grace and peace to you in fullest measure.

✻ 1. For an account of *Peter* see pp. 3 ff.

God's scattered people is a phrase borrowed from the Jews,
who used the term 'diaspora' (dispersion) to designate
Jewish people who lived outside Palestine; but it seems to be
applied here to the Christian church made up of all nations,
for the letter is not addressed only to Jewish Christians. They
lodge for a while because Christians are like those of old who
'died in faith' and thought of themselves as 'strangers or
passing travellers on earth', as Heb. 11: 13 expresses it. For
an explanation of the places where they lived, see p. 6 f. and
the map on p. 6.

2. *chosen of old in the purpose of God the Father*: It is a mistake
to draw the over-logical conclusion that when the New
Testament writers use such language they mean that God
has foreordained who shall be saved and who shall be lost.
Sometimes their language sounds like that and can be made
to say that; but their constant calling upon people to accept
the grace which God offers, and to use their own freewill to
live according to the new way which his grace has made
possible—these show that they mean something different.
This is that God has a plan for all men, that 'all men should

find salvation and come to know the truth' (I Tim. 2: 4). Thus Paul says that the disobedience of the Jews and their rejection of God's plan cannot frustrate his purpose, which is to 'show mercy to all mankind' (Rom. 9–11, esp. 11: 25–36). Again, Luke 7: 30 says that the Pharisees 'rejected God's purpose for themselves'. Because the sense of God's plan is so strong, sometimes thinkers in the New Testament go on to speak as if it were part of God's plan that men do wicked things and bring God's punishment on them; thus the betrayal of Jesus and his crucifixion is so regarded. Peter is represented in Acts 2: 23 as saying to the Jews in Jerusalem, that when Jesus had been given up to them 'by the deliberate will and plan of God, you used heathen men to crucify and kill him'. And Paul in Romans writes as though God were responsible for men disobeying him: 'he not only shows mercy as he chooses, but also makes men stubborn as he chooses' (Rom. 9: 18); nor does Paul extricate himself from the position in which these words place him. But we must judge not by these examples alone but by the general sense of the New Testament and the Christian gospel, which is that God has a plan for all men and that they sin when they reject it, having the choice to accept or reject. Here in I Peter the emphasis falls on the mercy of God, who 'chose' all those who accepted the gospel.

hallowed...by the Spirit: Heb. 9: 13 f. is the best commentary on this: the Jews felt the necessity for ceremonial cleanness when they had to perform some religious duty. 'The sprinkled ashes of a heifer have power to hallow those who have been defiled' (in this outward sense) 'and restore their external purity'. It is the Spirit of God which cleanses our inner selves from sin. The next verse in Hebrews (9: 14) says 'his blood will cleanse our conscience from the deadness of our former ways and fit us for the service of the living God'. In Exod. 24: 3–8 Moses sprinkled blood on the people as a sign that a covenant was being made between them and God. They could now come near to God and be his people. But sin keeps God and people apart, so there had to be a new covenant (which is another way of translating the words usually translated 'New Testament') and this new covenant offers to all people a way of approach to God by union with Christ. His death, the shedding of his blood, takes away the sin barrier, so we are *consecrated with the sprinkled blood of Jesus Christ*. In Old Testament times the actual blood was thought in some way to cleanse the worshippers ceremonially. The *blood of Jesus Christ* means his death, and his death consecrates us in an entirely different way from the old consecration by blood. The church has never settled on any one way as the right explanation of how this is true; but one very important aspect of it is that Christians in baptism by union with Christ 'die' to their old selves and begin a new life in union with the risen Christ. This is how they are consecrated.

Grace and peace: Christian version of the customary beginning of a secular letter, which after the names of the sender and the person addressed always had the word, 'Greetings!'

Before we go on to read and comment on this work, we must have some idea of the character of the main part, which so far we have called a sermon and which stretches from 1: 3 to 4: 11. It is certainly not misleading to call it a sermon, and it is just as reasonable to call it a sermon on baptism and the life to which it commits us. Everyone would agree to that, but some would go further and say that the sermon shows signs of the service in which it was delivered, and that it is more than a sermon—it is the whole liturgy, i.e. a form of service, with prayer and praise, used by a bishop when he was conducting a baptism. Further, since in the early days of the church baptism was carried out almost exclusively within the framework of the Paschal Eucharist (Easter Communion), this central part of I Peter can be considered a 'Paschal Liturgy'. We shall accept this idea in so far as it gives point to the different parts of the work. We shall find that, even if this theory is wrong, the fact that this section (1: 3 — 4: 11) is agreed to be a sermon on baptism and its duties and privileges means that such a way of looking at it, tentatively used, will make it clearer. Since baptism is the entrance to the Christian life, we may expect a sermon on the Christian life—and we shall not be disappointed if we are sensible enough to bear in mind that the author lived in a very different world from ours and expected that world to end soon. The right method is to look beyond the details of the time when he was living (though these have their own interest) to his principles and his understanding of the essence of the Christian life.

Analysis of the sermon will help to show that it does indeed contain some material, such as praise, to an extent abnormal in a sermon, together with teaching about baptism and the standards to which it commits all who accept it, demanding obedience to God in every part of life and patience under suffering.

1: 3 — 2: 10	*Christ and the People of God*
1: 3–12	Praise to God for his work in Christ
1: 13–21	Opening exhortation, perhaps to those about to be baptized
1: 22 — 2: 10	Exhortation to live worthily of the Christian calling in baptism, which has perhaps just taken place
2: 11 — 3: 12	*The obedience of a Christian man*
2: 11–25	Obedience in the world
3: 1–7	Obedience in marriage
3: 8–12	Summing up
3: 13 — 4: 11	*Suffering in Christ*
3:13–18*a*	The suffering of a Christian
3: 18*b*–22	(Digression: The disobedient spirits and baptism)
4: 1–11	New life in Christ ✳

I: 3 — 2: 10   CHRIST AND THE PEOPLE OF GOD
PRAISE TO GOD FOR HIS WORK IN CHRIST

Praise be to the God and Father of our Lord Jesus Christ, 3
who in his mercy gave us new birth into a living hope
by the resurrection of Jesus Christ from the dead! The 4
inheritance to which we are born is one that nothing can
destroy or spoil or wither. It is kept for you in heaven,
and you, because you put your faith in God, are under 5
the protection of his power until salvation comes—the
salvation which is even now in readiness and will be
revealed at the end of time.

This is cause for great joy, even though now you smart 6
for a little while, if need be, under trials of many kinds.
Even gold passes through the assayer's fire, and more 7
precious than perishable gold is faith which has stood the
test. These trials come so that your faith may prove
itself worthy of all praise, glory, and honour when Jesus
Christ is revealed.

You have not seen him, yet you love him; and trusting 8
in him now without seeing him, you are transported
with a joy too great for words, while you reap the harvest
of your faith, that is, salvation for your souls. This 9, 10
salvation was the theme which the prophets pondered
and explored, those who prophesied about the grace of
God awaiting you. They tried to find out what was the 11
time, and what the circumstances, to which the spirit
of Christ in them pointed, foretelling the sufferings in
store for Christ and the splendours to follow; and it 12
was disclosed to them that the matter they treated of
was not for their time but for yours. And now it has

been openly announced to you through preachers who brought you the Gospel in the power of the Holy Spirit sent from heaven. These are things that angels long to see into.

⁂ 3. *Praise be to the God and Father*: in the section on Worship in *Understanding the New Testament*, the introductory volume in this series, we see how the writings of the New Testament echo the worship of the church (pp. 88 ff); and Eph. 1: 3 ff.— 'Praise be to the God and Father of our Lord Jesus Christ, who has bestowed on us in Christ every spiritual blessing...' —is compared with our present passage. The opening words could be translated 'Blessed be...' and they reflect the standard form of Jewish blessing (*berakah*). God is the *Father of our Lord Jesus Christ* and our Father through our union with Christ.

gave us new birth into a living hope: verse 23, 'You have been born anew', echoes the idea of rebirth in connexion with baptism. The thought is found in several important places in the New Testament, as Rom. 6: 4, 'By baptism we were buried with him', and in the next verse, 'we shall also be one with him in a resurrection like his'. So also John 3: 3 and 5, 'no one can enter the kingdom of God without being born from water and spirit'; and Matt. 18: 3, 'unless you turn round and become like children, you will never enter the kingdom of Heaven'. In slightly different ways, each emphasizes the necessity of a new life. This is not a new life in the sense only of a life after this, but a new life of a different quality from the ordinary earthly life, which can be started now by entering on the way of union with Christ.

by the resurrection of Jesus Christ: this is the keystone of the gospel: not the historical details that the tomb was found empty and that the Lord appeared to his disciples, for these things might be explained away; but the conquest of death and evil which Christ communicates to his followers, a conquest which is a fact and continues to be a fact. It is sacramentally conveyed to the Christian by baptism into Christ.

4–5. *The inheritance*: Through the 'righteousness that came from' Abraham's 'faith' he received the promise that 'the world should be his inheritance' (Rom. 4: 13). In a Letter to Hebrews, Abraham is one of many who 'are commemorated for their faith and yet they did not enter upon the promised inheritance' (11: 39). The idea of *the inheritance* had been variously interpreted, some thinking it meant a country to live in, or a kingdom to enjoy, ruling over other peoples. Here it means the kingdom of God, the blessed state of the righteous when God at last reigns on the earth, either because Christ returns to reign, or because all men have been won to serve God.

kept for you in heaven: Almost the same phrase occurs in Col. 1: 5, 'stored up for you in heaven', meaning that it is part of the plan of God, a plan whose final feature *will be revealed at the end of time, the salvation* or victory of all who trust in Christ.

6–7. The argument here is clear: it is implied, though not stated, that the trials of Christians sort out those who are really full of faith from the others. Those who give up *under trials of many kinds* will prove to be not true gold and will not receive the inheritance. It is clear from the rest of 1 Peter that the author expects Christians to be subject to *trials*, as the author of a Letter of James did ('whenever you have to face trials of many kinds, count yourselves supremely happy', Jas. 1: 2). Our author shows that he lived at a time when 'pagans...malign' Christians 'as criminals' (2: 12) and this would be the source of many petty persecutions even when there was no organized persecution by the state. Jesus taught his followers to pray to be spared 'the test' (Matt. 6: 13), an alternative translation of the Greek word.

when Jesus Christ is revealed: As he had already been revealed in his earthly days, this obviously means 'at the end of time' (verse 5). It is important to remember all the time we read the New Testament that every word of it was written under the strong conviction that this event of the end of the age,

when Jesus would return as judge, was not far off. 1 Peter
thinks that it is 'upon us' (4: 7) and judgement is beginning
with the church itself (4: 17). For the true Christian, he insists,
this is cause for great joy, a joy he possesses already.

8. *You have not seen him, yet you love him...trusting in
him...without seeing him*: those addressed deserve the blessing
pronounced by Jesus in John 20: 29, 'Happy are they who
never saw me and yet have found faith'.

10–12. In Col. 1: 26 f. the author speaks of his task as 'to
announce the secret hidden for long ages and through many
generations, but now disclosed to God's people...' and there
is a very similar passage in Eph. 3: 2–6. There are a number
of passages which, like this, link 1 Peter with Colossians and
Ephesians. In the original Greek it is clear that the Ephesians
passage (4: 25, 31) is an elaboration of that in Colossians (3: 8),
and that 1 Peter is very like Ephesians, less like Colossians. It
seems therefore likely that the author of 1 Peter knew and
used Ephesians. It is also true that in other places there is
evidence for a common body of teaching used by all; this,
rather than the fact that one has copied the other, may account
for strong similarities. Explanation in terms of copying is
most likely at 2: 13 ff., where we meet teaching on duty to
the state. There 1 Peter has something significant in common
with Rom. 13: 1 ff. and the whole passage 2: 13 — 3: 7 finds
echoes in other parts of the New Testament, as is explained
in the commentary below.

10. *the prophets pondered and explored*: here is another very
important feature of the early church which will seem strange
to us. Once convinced that Jesus was the Messiah by his
resurrection, the first Christians searched the scriptures to
find indications that all that had happened to Jesus, including
his death and resurrection, had been foretold by the prophets.
To show this they sometimes gave a meaning to the scriptures
which they certainly did not originally bear. A famous
example of this is Paul's argument in Gal. 3: 16. God's
promises to 'Abraham's seed' in several places in Genesis,

e.g. 12: 7 and 17: 8, obviously meant his descendants in the plural. Paul says it meant Abraham's 'issue'—'and the "issue" intended is Christ'—'in the singular', as Paul says so definitely. No rabbi could object to this sort of argument, since it was the way in which rabbis habitually argued. We might declare that we must find out what the original writer meant and exclude all other interpretations; but in the days of the New Testament (and a long time before and after it) the firm belief that the scriptures were full of God's mysteries waiting for special gifts to unravel them made it not only possible but laudable to look for hidden meanings not seen before. The special Christian point of view was that everything pointed to the revelation in Jesus, and that this provided the key to the meaning of the scriptures.

11. *the spirit of Christ in them*: these words are a clue to another feature, and a developed one, of the doctrine about the scriptures just explained: it is that the story in the old scriptures (which Christians call the Old Testament) contains references to Christ himself. Since he existed before he was born as a human being ('the Word already was', John 1: 1, before 'the Word became flesh', John 1: 14), he must have been active in God's revelation under the old covenant. Thus Paul can speak of 'the supernatural rock that accompanied' the travels of the Israelites in the wilderness and add boldly—'and that rock was Christ' (1 Cor. 10: 4); and 1 Peter can say that it was *the spirit of Christ* in the prophets which spoke of the things to come, that is, *the sufferings in store for Christ and the splendours to follow*. In Luke 24: 25–7 and 46 we find the risen Jesus himself using the scriptures in this way. He rebuked the two disciples he met on the way to Emmaus for their dullness 'and explained to them the passages which referred to himself in every part of the scriptures'.

12. *preachers who brought you the Gospel*: the speaker or writer does not seem to count himself among these. The word 'brought' is not in the Greek, which does not necessarily imply that the hearers were being addressed from a distance.

things that angels long to see into: angels are often, in biblical literature, the intermediaries of revelation to mortals. Ezekiel is shown the ideal new temple by an angelic being in Ezek. 40: 3 ff.; and an angel interprets to Zechariah his vision in Zech. 1: 9 in a way recalled in Rev. 22: 6, where 'the angel who spoke with me' (Rev. 21: 15) says to the author, 'The Lord God who inspires the prophets has sent his angel to show his servants what must shortly happen.' The Palestinian Targum (a version of the Hebrew scriptures in Aramaic) comments on Jacob's ladder (Gen. 28: 12) that the holy angels had been desirous to see Jacob and they ascended and descended and looked at him. 1 Peter has the very similar thought that angels long to look into mysteries revealed on earth. Even the angels have not been granted the revelation *openly announced* to Christians. This revelation is the Christian Gospel, hinted at by the prophets under the guidance of the Holy Spirit, their meaning being only now clear. In Matt. 13: 17 and Luke 10: 24 Jesus says that the disciples are specially blessed because they see what great men of the past longed to see and did not see. A rather perverse interpretation of this made some believe later on that the disciples had been entrusted with secrets of the universe by Jesus which they afterwards revealed to others who wrote books bearing the names of the disciples; but the church did not accept their genuineness or authority. ✳

OPENING EXHORTATION, PERHAPS TO THOSE ABOUT TO BE BAPTIZED

13 You must therefore be like men stripped for action, perfectly self-controlled. Fix your hopes on the gift of grace which is to be yours when Jesus Christ is revealed.
14 As obedient children, do not let your characters be shaped any longer by the desires you cherished in your days of
15 ignorance. The One who called you is holy; like him, be

holy in all your behaviour, because Scripture says,
'You shall be holy, for I am holy.'   16

  If you say 'our Father' to the One who judges every   17
man impartially on the record of his deeds, you must
stand in awe of him while you live out your time on earth.
Well you know that it was no perishable stuff, like gold   18
or silver, that bought your freedom from the empty
folly of your traditional ways. The price was paid in   19
precious blood, as it were of a lamb without mark or
blemish—the blood of Christ. He was predestined before   20
the foundation of the world, and in this last period of
time he was made manifest for your sake. Through him   21
you have come to trust in God who raised him from the
dead and gave him glory, and so your faith and hope are
fixed on God.

✵ This section fits very well with the theory that the speaker
now turns from his praise to address those who are waiting
to receive baptism; but the passage also makes excellent sense
if we take it that he simply addresses Christians on the basis
of what he has just said and demands a high moral standard
from them.

  13. *stripped for action*: both men and women were in the early
church baptized almost naked, in separate groups; when they
came up out of the water they put on a new garment. This
signified the abandonment of the old and the adoption of the
new life, but the speaker here makes a different point; the
Christian must have 'the loins of his mind' girded (as the
author puts it here literally), as though stripped for action,
his undergarment tucked up out of the way. In Luke 12: 35 f.
Jesus urges the disciples in the time between his departure
and his return to 'be ready for action, with belts fastened'
(lit. 'with loins girded')...'Be like men who wait for their
master's return from a wedding-party...'

15–16. *like him, be holy*: The quotation '*You shall be holy, for I am holy*' is from Lev. 19: 2. This part of the Law gave detailed instruction on preserving and restoring ceremonial holiness so that a worshipper could approach God, or be readmitted to contact with the rest of society after becoming for one reason or another 'unclean'. In time Jews came to regard a sin as ceremonially defiling so that it must be put right in two ways; the necessary rite must be performed to restore ceremonial purity, and penitence must restore their inner purity. We do not as a rule understand what a great advance this was, since we regard religion and morality as closely linked or even as the same. But they are not the same, and for many minds are not even linked. The people of Qumran (a Jewish sect whose scriptures were found there on the north-west shore of the Dead Sea in 1947) show that they have recognized the inner defiling nature of sin although they are most strict on the necessity for ceremonial purification. So, too, John the Baptist baptized to cleanse from the ceremonial defilement; but he laid the greatest emphasis on the inner cleansing: 'prove your repentance by the fruit it bears', he insisted (Luke 3: 8). According to Mark 7: 18 ff. Jesus taught the very new doctrine that 'nothing that goes from outside into a man can defile him' and 'it is what comes out of a man that defiles him. For from inside, out of a man's heart, come evil thoughts, acts...' Peter, who is claimed to be the author of this letter, did not seem to have taken this in, as we have already seen in the note on the opening (p. 4), for he needed a special revelation to be persuaded of its truth (Acts 10: 9–16). Whether Peter finally understood this perfectly or not, the author of 1 Peter is very clear on the matter, for he understands holiness or purity as entirely moral. Although he is linking all his teaching to baptism, he insists that 'baptism is not the washing away of bodily pollution' (3: 21: see the note there). The point he is making is simple but great: just as in the old covenant a man must be holy in the ceremonial sense to be acceptable to God and to

24

be a member of God's people, so now he must be holy in the moral sense to be able to stand before the presence of the Christ of God when he 'is revealed' (verse 13).

17. The N.E.B. takes it that here is a reference to the Lord's Prayer, which is very likely. Even if this is not so, a Christian who dares to use the name of Father for the God who is to judge must not presume on this close relation bestowed on him by Christ; it is not enough to be holy when the day of judgement comes; *you must stand in awe of him while you live out your time on earth*. This is one way of making the Christian message of the New Testament, delivered under the belief that the judgement was imminent, relevant for us today; we are to live as if the judgement were imminent every day, while we *live out* our *time*, because we call God the judge our Father. This is not a reason for complacency, as the author goes on to argue, from a different point of view, in the next verse.

18–19. The unredeemed man is subject to fear of the gods: he offers sacrifices to propitiate their wrath but goes on still in a way of life which is *empty folly*. The author is addressing pagans or those from such a background: before baptism they are not God's people but aliens (2: 10 f.; cf. 4: 3 f.). Sin still stands in the way between the unredeemed man and God. See the note on 1: 2 where it was explained that Christ's blood was thought of as the blood making valid the new covenant by which a man can now approach God, the barrier of sin being taken away. In the past a man might pay for sacrifices to be offered on his behalf with *gold or silver;* but now God has himself *paid in precious blood*. Animals intended for sacrifice must according to Lev. 22: 17–25 be *without mark or blemish*, but there is probably here a special reference to Exod. 12: 5 which insists that the Passover Lamb must be 'without blemish'. We have seen that the work we are studying may be the liturgy, or at least a sermon for the Paschal Eucharist or Easter Communion; this was held at the time of Passover (Easter is still calculated with reference to the paschal moon) and many features of the Jewish Passover, the great Jewish festival of deliverance, were taken over into the Christian festival and offered themes for sermons at it. Thus it becomes very natural that Jesus should be thought of as the Paschal Lamb, *without mark or blemish*: this idea was strongly influenced by the belief that Jesus had been crucified at Passover time and so had been the means of a new 'exodus' or deliverance.

20. *He was predestined*: not only do Christians believe that 'the Word already was' before 'the Word became flesh' (John 1: 1 and 14) but that his suffering *was predestined before the foundation of the world*, as is implied here; this is the Jewish way of saying that it was always part of the eternal plan of God.

21. *trust in God who raised him from the dead and gave him glory*: the entire hope of Christians is based on this, that Jesus who was crucified as a common criminal was vindicated by God who raised him from the dead and 'set him on a throne', that is, made him unseen ruler over the universe. This was declared to all who will accept it by raising him from the dead. They therefore see that the death of Jesus was not just a death but a sacrifice, or rather the sacrifice which turns men to God, and that even the death of Jesus was part of God's plan. Thus Christians come to see that God is at work in Christ and *so* their *faith and hope are fixed on God*.

If it is right to see in the work we are reading a baptismal liturgy, then we might see here the point at which the people, 'stripped for action' and exhorted to 'be holy in all' their 'behaviour' (verses 13 and 16), go down into the water and are baptized. There they leave their old selves behind and emerge to put on a new life, a metaphor found often in the New Testament. In Rom. 13: 14 Paul says literally, 'Put on the Lord Jesus Christ', and in Gal. 3: 27, as the N.E.B. itself translates, 'Baptized into union with him, you have all put on Christ as a garment.' *

I: 22 — 2: IO   EXHORTATION TO LIVE A LIFE WORTHY
OF THE CHRISTIAN CALLING IN BAPTISM,
WHICH HAS PERHAPS JUST TAKEN PLACE

Now that by obedience to the truth you have purified 22
your souls until you feel sincere affection towards your
brother Christians, love one another whole-heartedly
with all your strength. You have been born anew, not of 23
mortal parentage but of immortal, through the living
and enduring word of God. For (as Scripture says)   24

> 'All mortals are like grass;
> All their splendour like the flower of the field;
> The grass withers, the flower falls;
> But the word of the Lord endures for evermore.'   25

And this 'word' is the word of the Gospel preached to you.

Then away with all malice and deceit, away with all **2**
pretence and jealousy and recrimination of every kind!
Like the new-born infants you are, you must crave for 2
pure milk (spiritual milk, I mean), so that you may thrive
upon it to your souls' health. Surely you have tasted that 3
the Lord is good.

So come to him, our living Stone—the stone rejected 4
by men but choice and precious in the sight of God.
Come, and let yourselves be built, as living stones, into a 5
spiritual temple; become a holy priesthood, to offer
spiritual sacrifices acceptable to God through Jesus Christ.
For it stands written: 6

> 'I lay in Zion a choice corner-stone of great worth.
> The man who has faith in it will not be put to
>   shame.'

7 The great worth of which it speaks is for you who have faith. For those who have no faith, the stone which the builders rejected has become not only the corner-stone,

8 but also 'a stone to trip over, a rock to stumble against'. They stumble when they disbelieve the Word. Such was their appointed lot!

9 But you are a chosen race, a royal priesthood, a dedicated nation, and a people claimed by God for his own, to proclaim the triumphs of him who has called

10 you out of darkness into his marvellous light. You are now the people of God, who once were not his people; outside his mercy once, you have now received his mercy.

22–3. Note the tenses, *you have purified* ... and *you have been born anew*. If the baptism has taken place since the words spoken in verse 21, these phrases refer directly to this fact. If we are to understand the work as a discourse on the Christian life not connected with a baptism now actually taking place, it is still certain that the speaker is thinking of the baptism of the Christians whom he addresses, although each may have been baptized at a different time from the others. The action of undertaking the Christian life is called here *obedience to the truth*. *The truth* is the Gospel, which claims to be a revelation about God and his relation to man, not merely a system of moral exhortation. Paul saw that if a man accepted the Gospel it could be said of him that he 'believed'—a word he uses to mean to accept baptism and become a Christian in Rom. 13: 11 (N.E.B. 'when first we believed', but 'first' is not in the Greek)—but also that because the Gospel demanded to be believed since it was God's word, to accept it could also be called 'obedience'. Thus in Rom. 1: 5 he sees the work given him by God as the promotion of 'faith and obedience' among all men, and in 2 Cor. 10: 5 it is 'every human thought'

28

(i.e. all human beliefs and philosophies) which must 'surrender in obedience to Christ'.

You have been born anew: Paul thinks of baptism as a death and a new life; John, in the story about Nicodemus in John 3, and 1 Peter think of it as rebirth. See the note on 1: 3 where some references are given. *Mortal parentage* (literally, corruptible or mortal seed) is contrasted with birth through the *word*. This extends our understanding of the ancient rite of baptism, for it was never practised without the word, i.e. the Gospel, being closely connected with it. In the first place, in contrast to a purely 'religious' ceremony such as pagans might carry out, in which the will and mind of the person concerned were not engaged at all, Jewish or Christian baptism is the result of hearing and believing and obeying the word or Gospel preached, and therefore signifies acceptance of the Gospel. In the second place, it is carried out in close connexion with a sacred word uttered by the person being baptized, a word or phrase which is both sacred and at the same time very much his own word, because he utters it from the heart: this is some such formula as 'I believe Jesus is the Christ' or 'Jesus is Lord'. This word is not confined to the baptism ceremony but becomes the treasure of the Christian in his heart and the centre of his faith and life. It is to this that Paul refers with deep feeling in a passage which contains some elements difficult to understand but is crystal clear on this point. In Rom. 10: 9 he says, 'If on your lips is the confession, "Jesus is Lord", and in your heart the faith that God raised him from the dead, then you will find salvation.'

24–5. The quotation in verse 24 is from Isa. 40: 6–8, in which the unknown prophet insists that the word which he is proclaiming is certain to be fulfilled. Paul, in the passage of Romans just referred to, boldly takes a reference in Deut. 30:14 to 'the word' (where it means the commandment of God) to mean the word 'Jesus is Lord' uttered from and in the heart by a Christian. Equally boldly, 1 Peter claims that the prophet's 'word of the Lord' *is the word of the Gospel preached to you.*

These are two further examples of the bold use of scripture which we have met before.

2: 1–2. Rabbis compared *milk* to the Law, and later Christian writers compared it to the teaching given to converts to Christianity; but it is just possible that there is a reference to a baptismal custom here. We cannot say that such a custom obtained at the time 1 Peter was written, but we know from Hippolytus of Rome (*c.* 170–236) that in his time the person baptized received three cups in succession: of water, of milk, and of wine.

3. *Surely you have tasted that the Lord is good*: this reference to Ps. 34: 8 ('O taste and see that the Lord is good'), means something like 'You have tasted milk at your baptism, which is a good drink; but you have also received the Lord and he "tastes" better still'. This would be a reference to the bread and wine of the eucharist as well as to the milk, but above all to the Lord himself received in a spiritual sense.

4–8. *So come to him*: the invitation is not pious rhetoric but to those who are leaving one society (or claim to have left it) to join another (or to remind them to regard themselves as having joined another). This society is that of the People of God, thought of under the figure of a temple of which Christ is the chief stone and all Christians are the other stones.

A number of metaphors and ideas are mixed here and analysis of them will go far to explain the passage:

(*a*) *The stone* as a foundation. Isa. 28: 14–17 suggests that perhaps it was the Lord God who was first spoken of as a trustworthy stone in contrast to others which would afford neither shelter nor foundation in a day when trouble came. This idea of a stone which will stand fast was early transferred from God to be applied to Zion itself, as it is in Isa. 28: 16, quoted in verse 6 here, and Rom. 9: 33. In Isa. 8: 14 f., which is also used in this passage, the Lord is a sure sanctuary but at the same time is

(*b*) '*a stone to trip over, a rock to stumble against*' for those who are unfaithful to him. *They stumble when they disbelieve* (so verse 8 here).

(c) *the stone rejected by men but choice and precious in the sight of God* (verse 4) was no doubt originally Israel, as in Ps. 118: 22 ('the stone which the builders rejected'), but it was interpreted in Christian circles as referring to Jesus the rejected Messiah, and may have been so used by Jesus himself, for it is added as if spoken by him at the end of the story of the wicked farmers at Mark 12: 10. Thus Jesus the Messiah is thought of as the *living Stone*.

(d) *a spiritual temple*, a notion with a long history and whose many forms we are only just beginning to appreciate to the full. The basic idea is that the Jerusalem temple and its system of worship and sacrifice needed to be replaced because they had been defiled both by the pollution caused by the setting up of a heathen altar under Antiochus Epiphanes in 168 B.C. and by the high priesthood being held by unworthy and unqualified persons. The men of Qumran were so certain that the priesthood must be replaced that they went out into the desert to build up a community which would replace the temple by a community of the faithful. Their way of being faithful meant rigid adherence to the Law in all circumstances, including persecution. The Christian church, on the other hand, believed that the temple and its sacrifices had been replaced once for all by Jesus and the fellowship round the risen Lord. Qumran and the early church were the only two groups of whom we know who believed in and implemented this conception of a spiritual temple to replace that of stone. The main passage in the Dead Sea Scrolls (from Qumran) is in the *Rule* (or *Manual of Discipline*) 8: 4 ff. which speaks of the new community as 'a trusty wall, a precious cornerstone'. In the New Testament the idea of a temple made up of the people of God is found in a number of places, including Paul in 1 Cor. 3: 16, 'Surely you know that you are God's temple, where the Spirit of God dwells', implying that the Corinthians had been taught this long ago; and when in 2 Cor. 6: 16 Paul wants to insist on the special character of God's people as holy he asks, 'Can there be a compact between the temple of God and the idols of the heathen?' Again, in the strange passage in John 2, Jesus says he will raise again 'this temple' if it is destroyed (2: 19) and John adds that 'the temple he was speaking of was his body' (2: 21).

(*e*) *a holy priesthood*—another idea shared with the men of Qumran, who not only gave a place of honour to priests in their community but enjoined on lay members rules of purity which in the Law had been laid down for officiating priests; thus their ideal was for the whole community so to keep the regulations of the ancient Law that they could be regarded corporately as a holy priesthood. But the idea was already in the Law, for in Exod. 19: 6 God says, 'ye shall be unto me a kingdom of priests, and an holy nation'.

(*f*) An idea which is perhaps obvious, that of a *spiritual* priesthood in a *spiritual* temple offering *spiritual* sacrifices. At Qumran the sacrificial system was 'spiritualized' by being replaced by a careful keeping of the Law; in the church it is spiritualized by the offering of the whole life and self of the Christian in union with Christ to the service of God.

9. The author then summons Christians to regard their baptism as bringing them in 'as living stones' to build up the 'spiritual temple' which is elsewhere called the Body of Christ. They will thus be united to the member of the Body or building who is the most important stone of it, though originally rejected; and they will thus make up a spiritual temple which replaces that made of actual stone and be a *chosen race, a royal priesthood, a dedicated nation*. Each comes *out of darkness into . . . light*. To be 'enlightened' often meant to have become a Christian through baptism (as in Heb. 6: 4). See the hymn at Eph. 5: 14 ('Christ will shine upon you').

10. The prophet Hosea had given expression to his sense of the sin and pathos of the situation in which Israel, bride of Yahweh, had been unfaithful to the Lord; he did this by calling his daughter Lo-ruhamah, i.e. 'No-mercy' (1: 6) and his son Lo-ammi, i.e. 'Not-my-people' (1: 9). This verse plays upon

32

these facts, as does Paul in Rom. 9: 25, 'Those who were not my people I will call My People . . .' Paul makes those who were previously no people of God, but who have now become so, mean the Gentiles; 1 Peter on the other hand seems to have in mind all converts, whether Jews or Gentiles, before they became Christians. ✻

2: 11 — 3: 12   THE OBEDIENCE OF A CHRISTIAN MAN

✻ 2: 11–12 are introductory. At 2: 13, with the words 'Submit yourselves,' a section of the work, 2: 13 — 3: 7, is introduced which contains or adapts parts of one or more social codes. These, drawn up to govern different departments of life, were current in both Jewish and hellenistic circles. It seems that early Christians composed their own, perhaps modelled on some already existing; they are found incorporated in various books of the New Testament (see below).

Here it seems that we have a comprehensive code of subordination. This is its teaching:

(*a*) 2: 13–17, obedience to civic authorities. Rom. 13: 1–7; 1 Tim. 2: 1–8; Titus 3: 1 show clear parallels.

(*b*) 2: 18–25, obedience of slaves to masters, found certainly also at Col. 3: 22–5; Eph. 6: 5–8; 1 Tim. 6: 1 f.; Titus 2: 9 f., but here in 1 Peter it is much more than a rule, for the obedience of the slave is taken as the type of the Christian life.

(*c*) 3: 1–6, obedience of wives to husbands, also at Col. 3: 18; Eph. 5: 22–4, where it is the model for the church's relation to Christ; Titus 2: 4 f.

(*d*) 3: 7, duties of husbands towards wives. That husbands have such duties is a mark of Jewish and Christian thought. See Col. 3: 19; Eph. 5: 25–33, where it is elaborated from a doctrinal point of view.

3: 8–12 is a conclusion. ✻

33

2: 11–25   OBEDIENCE IN THE WORLD

CHRISTIAN CITIZENS

11 Dear friends, I beg you, as aliens in a foreign land, to abstain from the lusts of the flesh which are at war with
12 the soul. Let all your behaviour be such as even pagans can recognize as good, and then, whereas they malign you as criminals now, they will come to see for themselves that you live good lives, and will give glory to God on the day when he comes to hold assize.

✶ 11. *aliens in a foreign land* reminds us of 'people who lodge for a while' in 1: 1 (see the note there). Christians belong to Christ through their baptism, and therefore to heaven. The author uses words from Ps. 39: 12 ('I am a stranger with thee') to express a thought which we saw was to be found also in Heb. 11: 13 ('strangers or passing travellers on earth'). 'We ... are citizens of heaven', says Paul in Phil. 3: 20. Christians have to live in two worlds. If they give way to *the lusts of the flesh* (greediness, drunkenness, uncontrolled sexual behaviour) they will be tied to this world and not allow *the soul* to be guided by the Spirit. After contrasting the two ways of life in Gal. 5: 19–25, where 'the flesh' is rightly translated by 'the lower nature', Paul there concluded: 'If the Spirit is the source of our life, let the Spirit also direct our course.' That is also the lesson here, and the language is downright. Like every writer in the New Testament, our author teaches a strict standard for everyday life. It should be understood that nowhere in the teaching of Jesus or anyone else in the New Testament is the natural life of the body condemned. In 1 Pet. 3: 1–7, married life is regarded a normal, and those who forbid others to marry are condemned as wrong in 1 Tim. 4: 1–3.

12. We know from Tacitus (*Annals* 15: 44) and Suetonius (*Claudius* 25 and *Nero* 16) of absurd and scandalous idea

about Christians in those early days; Tacitus speaks of 'abominations' committed by Christians and believes that Pontius Pilatus checked only temporarily 'a most mischievous superstition', which he classes among the 'hideous and shameful' things to be found in Rome. Suetonius also speaks of Christianity as 'a new and mischievous superstition'. Tertullian even had to meet the charge that Christians indulged secretly in cannibalism. I Peter counsels the removal of these absurd ideas by constant Christian behaviour. This is not only for the sake of the church but for God's *glory*, just as Jesus in Matt. 5: 16 wants Christians to be a light for all the world 'so that, when they see the good you do, they may give praise to your Father in heaven'. ✳

OBEDIENCE TO CIVIC AUTHORITIES

Submit yourselves to every human institution for the sake of the Lord, whether to the sovereign as supreme, or to the governor as his deputy for the punishment of criminals and the commendation of those who do right. For it is the will of God that by your good conduct you should put ignorance and stupidity to silence. 13 14 15

Live as free men; not however as though your freedom were there to provide a screen for wrongdoing, but as slaves in God's service. Give due honour to everyone: love to the brotherhood, reverence to God, honour to the sovereign. 16 17

✳ 13. *every human institution* includes the state. Christians are to obey it as part of their way of life (for the sake of the Lord). Jesus's own words in Mark 12: 13–17, 'Pay Caesar what is due to Caesar, and pay God what is due to God', may be the inspiration for this attitude. Paul's version in Rom. 13: 1–7 is fuller, going so far as to say there that 'the existing authorities are instituted by' God. If it seems strange to us that Paul and

the author of 1 Peter should be so sure that the state had the
authority of God, and if we are tempted to think that they
could have thought thus only in a time of peace when the
state was benevolent, it is well to reflect that both Paul and
the author of 1 Peter had good reason to fear at least the
severity of a state which did not understand what Christianity
was, and perhaps its real hostility. The unexpectedness of the
teaching is then something to be faced. It probably arises
from a very close acquaintance with the stern facts of political
life in Palestine, where fanatical Zealots who opposed the
Roman government on religious grounds often acted like
indiscriminate assassins, where Jews and Samaritans were
bitterly hostile to one another ('a Samaritan village...would
not' allow Jesus to stay there, for example, 'because he was
making for Jerusalem', Luke 9: 53) and various factions
disagreed even within more moderate Judaism. Paul probably
reflects the view of moderate Pharisees, and Jesus agreed with
it to the extent of believing that God had given the government of the land to the Romans, though they were of course
responsible to him for it. This is shown in John 19: 11 when
Jesus says to Pilate, 'You would have no authority at all over
me,...if it had not been granted you from above'. When the
state demands 'what is due to God', then it has to be resisted
but it is not its legitimate work of governing which has to be
resisted. This teaching was evidently part of a code of behaviour
for Christians given consistently in the churches. Titus is told
to 'remind them' of it in Titus 3: 1. The *right* of verse 14 and
good conduct of verse 15 refer to behaviour towards a neighbour
here the pagan. The conduct does not imply the good deed
commended by the rabbis, which were directed towards the
poor and others unable themselves to fulfil the Law's require-
ments (e.g. providing decent burial for pauper dead), nor
the good works of later Christian theology which would
atone for post-baptismal faults; but good deeds open to
public view, directed to society in general. The conception
is Greek: the advice is given on the basis of the need to win

better name for Christians, and is not in itself an explanation of the truly Christian ethic, even though Christian ideas are introduced. Even though it is largely motivated by common prudence, it does nevertheless tend to the furtherance of the gospel, and not the advantage of the individual. In verse 17 *the brotherhood* is the church, *the sovereign* is the emperor. ✵

CHRISTIAN SERVANTS

Servants, accept the authority of your masters with all due submission, not only when they are kind and considerate, but even when they are perverse. For it is a fine thing if a man endure the pain of undeserved suffering because God is in his thoughts. What credit is there in fortitude when you have done wrong and are beaten for it? But when you have behaved well and suffer for it, your fortitude is a fine thing in the sight of God.

18
19
20

✵ Most servants were what we should call slaves, and the institution of slavery was so much part of the social system in the Roman Empire that it could not be altered suddenly. No one thought of changing the system, but Christians earnestly desired to change the spirit in which it was worked. In Col. 4: 1 Paul orders: 'Masters, be just and fair to your slaves, knowing that you too have a Master in heaven.' Eph. 6: 9 tells masters, 'Give up using threats; remember you both have the same Master in heaven, and he has no favourites' —meaning that the status of master and slave is for this world only and God will judge all as slaves, or servants. It is indeed this very idea that the Christian should regard himself as a slave of God which probably prevented for a long time the rise of any doctrine that slavery was in itself wrong. It was no thought of that kind, but rather the insistence that before God all were equal which was the Christian teaching on the matter; a teaching characteristic of a group of people convinced of the imminent end of the age. It was the worship side by side of master and slave, and their partaking of the Holy Communion together, making them feel that 'we were all brought into one body by baptism' (1 Cor. 12: 13) and that 'there is no such thing as...slave and freeman...in Christ Jesus' (Gal. 3: 28), which undermined the institution of slavery and led at last to its abolition. Paul's famous letter to Philemon, asking him to forgive his slave Onesimus for running away, and to receive him back 'as a dear brother' (Philem. 16), is a clear example of this spirit at work.

This passage shows how the status of a slave seemed to the writer an opportunity to be like Christ; the following passage, verses 21-5, looks at the matter from the opposite point of view and compares Christ to a slave, who indeed, according to Phil. 2: 7, 'made himself nothing, assuming the nature of a slave'. A very high standard of service is demanded here. Not only is being a servant thought of as a vocation, but suffering undeservedly—which seems to be regarded as inevitable for a slave—is regarded as an opportunity of pleasing God. Evidently even pagan masters were to be obeyed—and endured. *

CHRIST THE EXAMPLE AS SERVANT AND SUFFERER

21 To that you were called, because Christ suffered on your behalf, and thereby left you an example; it is for
22 you to follow in his steps. He committed no sin, he was
23 convicted of no falsehood; when he was abused he did not retort with abuse, when he suffered he uttered no threats, but committed his cause to the One who judges
24 justly. In his own person he carried our sins to the gallows, so that we might cease to live for sin and begin to live for righteousness. By his wounds you have been healed.
25 You were straying like sheep, but now you have turned towards the Shepherd and Guardian of your souls.

✻ 21. *To that you were called*, that is, to the undeserved suffering whose patient endurance is commended in the previous verse. This is a central theme of the work; that to be Christian means to suffer, often undeservedly.

Christ suffered: the versions which say '*died*' are probably to be explained by the wish of the scribe writing out the manuscript to be more exact or to make the passage more like others about Christ's sacrifice. *Suffered* is a term used of martyrs, and to say, as in the Creed, that Christ 'suffered under Pontius Pilate' means that he actually gave his life, not merely that he suffered in a general sense. He is the supreme example of a martyr for those willing to witness, or be a martyr, to him. Verse 24 below says more about the important words *on your behalf*. Here the point is that he left *an example* especially appropriate for slaves who suffer unjustly.

22. The words come from Isa. 53: 9 and are another example of the use of Scripture by the early church. The theme is not elaborated enough for us to say that the author sees Christ here as a fulfilment of the whole picture of the Suffering Servant drawn in the famous passage Isa. 52: 13 — 53: 12. It is a relatively isolated text which is thought of as being fulfilled rather than the whole picture.

23. *when he suffered he uttered no threats* as did many victims of this barbarous punishment to those who carried it out.

24. *he carried our sins* are words borrowed from Isa. 53: 4, but the idea is developed in relation to the crucifixion. The N.E.B. says *to the gallows* and in the footnote suggests that this could be 'on the gallows'. Perhaps the sense could be conveyed by the not very good English of 'up on to', for the idea seems to be that Christ was the representative of the whole human race and so all its sins could be thought of as concentrated on *his own person*. If then he carried them up in his person on to the cross, they were there put to death in him. By identifying with him we could thus see our sins 'put to death' *so that we might cease to live for sin and begin to live for righteousness*. This is why *by his wounds you have been healed*, words taken

from Isa. 53: 5. Paul's use of the same idea in Col. 2: 14 is less direct; there what is thought of as being 'nailed to the cross' is a bond (a legal document of binding force which implied that all men were liable to punishment).

25. *You were straying like sheep* reflects Isa. 53: 6. Christ is of course *the Shepherd and Guardian*, the first comparison being a constant thought of John's Gospel. Both authors are largely concerned with the idea of the gathering of God's people whose leader is compared to a shepherd, while those who scatter, causing strife and division, are called 'wolves'. Bad pastors of the church had evidently been known, for John makes Jesus refer to 'the hireling' who, 'when he sees the wolf coming, abandons the sheep and runs away' (John 10: 12). This reflects the time of the early church, as does the speech uttered by Paul, according to Acts 20: 18 ff., at Miletus; he appeals to the 'elders of the congregation' (Acts 20: 17) 'to keep watch... over all the flock...as shepherds of the church of the Lord, which he won for himself by his own blood' (Acts 20: 28). In a fight with the enemy a shepherd may give his own life to save the flock in his care. This is used as a further figure of speech about Jesus, who in John 10: 11 says, 'I am the good shepherd; the good shepherd lays down his life for the sheep.' Paul thinks further: by the resurrection, the shepherd in this case has 'won' the flock, for they are restored to him and he to them. This seems to be part of the thought of both John and 1 Peter: in the former, the risen Jesus tells Peter to 'feed' his 'lambs' and his 'sheep' (John 21: 15–17), and 1 Pet. 5: 1 ff. passes on the same command with the same figure of speech to 'the elders of' the 'community'. The word here translated *guardian* means literally overseer, and is the word which later gave us 'bishop'. Paul uses the word only once in his letters: in Phil. 1: 1 he addresses the 'bishops and deacons'. The order which came to stand between the deacon (usually a young man at the beginning of his ministry) and the bishop was that which is called 'elders' at 1 Pet. 5: 1. This is an exact translation of the Greek word which has sometimes been

transliterated into 'presbyters', of which the English 'priests' is a derived form. Paul does not mention elders in his letters; the speech in Acts 20: 18 ff. implies that they are exactly the same as 'bishops', which is the word translated 'shepherds' in verse 28, and is used of the same men as were summoned as elders in verse 17. This agrees with the Pastoral Letters of Timothy and Titus, for Titus 1: 5 ff. seems to identify bishops and elders. Here there is no question of a technical use of terms, and *guardian* brings out well the force of the word in this context. *

OBEDIENCE IN MARRIAGE

In the same way you women must accept the authority 3 of your husbands, so that if there are any of them who disbelieve the Gospel they may be won over, without a word being said, by observing the chaste and reverent 2 behaviour of their wives. Your beauty should reside, not 3 in outward adornment—the braiding of the hair, or jewellery, or dress—but in the inmost centre of your 4 being, with its imperishable ornament, a gentle, quiet spirit, which is of high value in the sight of God. Thus it 5 was among God's people in days of old: the women who fixed their hopes on him adorned themselves by submission to their husbands. Such was Sarah, who obeyed 6 Abraham and called him 'my master'. Her children you have now become, if you do good and show no fear.

In the same way, you husbands must conduct your 7 married life with understanding: pay honour to the woman's body, not only because it is weaker, but also because you share together in the grace of God which gives you life. Then your prayers will not be hindered.

* We cannot rightly derive Christian teaching about marriage from a passage such as this without very considerable

allowance for the situation in which it was written and the sequence of thought of the author, together with the background of his thinking. He is dominated by the idea of the quiet acceptance of a subservient position for the wife as an imitation of Christ. That is why he continues with the words, *In the same way.* A wife obeying her husband may be such an example no less than the patient slave. In the West we might well shrug off such an idea as impossible, but in the East it would still not be in the least remarkable, because in many countries the position in society is the same as is taken for granted in 1 Peter and the parallel passages, Col. 3: 18, Eph. 5: 22–4; 1 Tim. 2: 9–15; Titus 2: 4 f. A woman who made herself equal to her husband would be regarded as 'fast', and it was usually only in those pagan religions with immoral ceremonies that women were prominent in a religious community. Behind these unexamined and unspoken thoughts there lies the assumption that God created Adam first, and that Eve, the first woman, owed her existence to him and to his need for a helper (Gen. 2: 18); although a profounder interpretation was current which saw Adam before Eve was taken out of his side as a bi-sexual creature, implying that man and woman were partners rather than master and helper. There is no sign of this idea here.

1–2. *accept the authority of your husbands*: the author believed this was a law laid down by God for all marriages, for God had said to Eve in Gen. 3: 16 'he shall rule over thee'. If we take the story in Genesis as a myth we may well think of it as a descriptive rather than a prescriptive myth, i.e. it tells us how things are, not necessarily how things should be. But we must give the author credit for his insight into the fact that men *may be won over* by their wives' *chaste and reverent behaviour.* A modern Christian may reject the notion that woman is to adopt a permanent position of inferiority to man, but cannot reject that such behaviour as is described here may well make a profound impression on a man *without a word being said.* 'Submission to...husbands' (verse 5) is

42

here recommended as the true adornment of wives and as the way to win them to the faith. This seems to be a special application of what was taught consistently in the churches, but originally based on doctrine and enjoined for a doctrinal reason. Thus in Col. 3: 18 f. this subjection is described as the wives' 'Christian duty' and does not sound doctrinal. It may be the full teaching underlying all the passages on this subject which we find in Eph. 5: 22 f.: 'Wives, be subject to your husbands as to the Lord; for the man is the head of the woman, just as Christ also is the head of the church.' The point about true adornment is made again in 1 Tim. 2: 9, supporting the view that there was a stock sermon or sermon-ette on the subject repeated in the churches. The 1 Timothy passage indeed adds a highly doctrinal and rather obscure part (verses 13–15) which begins clearly enough and shows the Old Testament basis of this teaching about husband and wife: 'For Adam was created first, and Eve afterwards; and it was not Adam who was deceived; it was the woman...'

6. Sarah was not notable for her submissive spirit, and the use of the term 'my master' in Gen. 18: 12 in the Hebrew does not imply more than 'my husband' or 'the master of the house'. The word used in the Greek version of Genesis might suggest 'master' or 'lord' and the author takes advantage of this. Sarah is used as the example because as Abraham's wife she was the traditional mother of God's people and symbolically in a special way of women proselytes. The wives addressed will be her true *children* if they follow her example.

if you do good and show no fear: Prov. 3: 25, echoed here, seems also to be in mind at verse 14 where the situation envisaged is one of persecution. It is an exhortation, therefore, to be brave in the face of threats and it seems that the author has chiefly in mind wives with husbands 'who disbelieve the Gospel' (verse 1) and may ill-treat their Christian wives for having accepted the despised and hated faith.

7. *In the same way, you husbands*: although the author does not mean *in the same way* to imply that there might be

occasions when a husband ought to submit to his wife (such an idea would not enter his head), this passage is a significant contribution to the more humane influence of Jewish and Christian ideas. The use of *understanding* in the marriage relation, whether it is the specifically sexual relation or the whole scope of marriage which is being considered, is an advance on the pagan concept which allowed a husband to regard his wife as his property. A Christian must remember that not only his own body but also *the woman's* (i.e. his wife's) *body* is a vessel (in the Greek *the woman's body* is called 'the weaker vessel') which can receive *the grace of God*. In other words, if human beings be thought of figuratively as receptacles ('vessels') to hold God's grace, a woman is as suitable as a man for this purpose. Christians have not paid enough attention to this notion of the human body ('honour God in your body' says Paul in 1 Cor. 6: 20) as the receiver of grace from God, and for this reason to be respected; but the plea for the use of *understanding* includes a plea for restraint in the sexual relation. ✳

SUMMING UP

8 To sum up: be one in thought and feeling, all of you; be full of brotherly affection, kindly and humble-minded.

9 Do not repay wrong with wrong, or abuse with abuse; on the contrary, retaliate with blessing, for a blessing is the inheritance to which you yourselves have been called.

10   'Whoever loves life and would see good days
       Must restrain his tongue from evil
       And his lips from deceit;

11   Must turn from wrong and do good,
       Seek peace and pursue it.

12   For the Lord's eyes are turned towards the righteous,
       His ears are open to their prayers;
       But the Lord's face is set against wrong-doers.'

* Here the ethical teaching, founded upon the situation of the slave unjustly treated and bearing it patiently, is expressed simply and loftily. Once again it is easy to see that this is not the idea of the author only but that he is expressing the teaching of the church of his day, in this case almost certainly going back to that of Jesus himself. Paul in 1 Thess. 4: 1–12 has a similar passage which, like this in 1 Peter, follows an appeal for restraint and honour in the life of the body with a general appeal for a high ethic in dealings with one's fellow-men. He shows by his words, 'you are yourselves taught by God to love one another, and you are...practising this rule of love ...' (1 Thess. 4: 9 f.) that he too was giving the teaching of the church. He has similar teaching in Rom. 12 (especially verse 17, 'Never pay back evil for evil'). Most people will be able without guidance to quote the words of Jesus which are of the same kind. They may be found in Matt. 5: 39 or Luke 6: 29.

The quotation in verses 10–12 is from Ps. 34: 12–16. It is typical of Paul to clinch the argument of a long passage with an extended quotation from Scripture, but this is usually in the form of a chain of passages from different books which all support the theme he has been urging on his readers. He does this at the end of the argument in Romans, at 15: 9–12, before he rounds off the letter with personal matters. Here 1 Peter gives a continuous passage which at first sight seems to be merely an exhortation to do good, but verse 11 (which is verse 14 of the psalm) does imply the necessity of not meeting evil with evil. For in real life we are faced with moral choice not at the beginning of the day when we are alone and imagine that we can choose today to do either good or evil, but when someone provokes us and we are there and then tempted to respond with evil. 1 Peter knows well that, for a Christian to make the choice of responding with good then, he must fix his 'hopes on the gift of grace' (1: 13) and be reborn (1: 23)—this is the Christian basis for conduct better than the usual conduct of the world. The world in general would not regard rendering evil for evil as worthy of blame, though Plato had condemned it long before, and other non-Christian thinkers saw that to do evil to the bad man may make him worse, and therefore is wrong. ✲

3: 13 — 4: 11   SUFFERING IN CHRIST
THE SUFFERING OF A CHRISTIAN

13 Who is going to do you wrong if you are devoted to
14 what is good? And yet if you should suffer for your
15 virtues, you may count yourselves happy. Have no fear of them: do not be perturbed, but hold the Lord Christ in reverence in your hearts. Be always ready with your defence whenever you are called to account for the hope that is in you, but make that defence with modesty and
16 respect. Keep your conscience clear, so that when you are abused, those who malign your Christian conduct may
17 be put to shame. It is better to suffer for well-doing, if such should be the will of God, than for doing wrong.
18a For Christ also died for our sins once and for all. He, the just, suffered for the unjust, to bring us to God.

✲ 13. *Who is going to do you wrong*... that such a question should be asked is strange, since the author has shown himself well aware of the sufferings which may befall anyone unjustly. Paul, too, in Rom. 13: 3, after his experiences at Philippi (Acts 16: 19–40), when he was flogged at the orders of Roman magistrates, and at Corinth (Acts 18: 12–17), when the proconsul was left 'quite unconcerned' at the beating of Paul's fellow-worker Sosthenes, could write: '...government, a terror to crime, has no terrors for good behaviour.' Here too the very next sentence shows that the author knows that the answer to his question is quite unfavourable to his argument. Probably the explanation is that both Paul and our

46

author held fast to the teaching that government has divine authority and overlooked its manifest mistakes as exceptions.

14–18. A return to the real subject, suffering *for virtues*. Here is plain teaching, very hard to obey, on how a Christian should endure persecution, reflecting the beatitude in Matt. 5: 10, 'How blest are those who have suffered persecution for the cause of right' (the same Greek word is translated *virtues* here). The key to it is in the words *hold the Lord Christ in reverence in your hearts*. This kind of silent prayer is akin to that which is implied by Paul in Rom. 10:9, though he is not there speaking necessarily of a situation in which the Christian is being persecuted: 'If on your lips is the confession, "Jesus is Lord", and in your heart the faith that God raised him from the dead, then you will find salvation.' The early church experienced the help of the Holy Spirit in such circumstances, as is clear from Mark 13: 11, 'It will not be you that speak, but the Holy Spirit', for these words of Jesus are not likely to have been recorded unless they had been found true. It is strange that the teaching of Jesus in the passage from Mark just mentioned, not to prepare defence beforehand, is here contradicted with the words *Be always ready with your defence*. Christians, when true to the teaching of their Lord and their church, make their *defence with modesty and respect*, not accusing their accusers but explaining their position as well as they can to those who are probably determined not to understand it. This demeanour has had the effect of converting many persecutors in different ages, not least in the twentieth century when opposers of Christianity in various countries have regarded Christians as enemies of the state, as the ancient Roman empire did at times.

16. *Keep your conscience clear* seems obvious advice, but it is the guilty conscience which weakens its defence even if not accused of the matters which cause the guilt. Jesus was able to be silent before his accusers because he had nothing on his conscience. We may not agree that *it is better to suffer for well-doing...than for doing wrong* but it is a point of view which

ought to be taken very seriously and perhaps debated. Many would say that it makes sense only in 'the eschatological situation'—that is, when the sufferers are expecting divine deliverance and vindication almost hourly, and when their sufferings are thought to be a way of entrance into God's rapidly approaching eternal kingdom. The author of 1 Peter believed this, and also that such suffering was inevitable for those who had united themselves to Christ.

18a. *Christ...died for our sins once and for all*: there is no easy way of explaining how the death of Christ can be regarded as effective for the removal of the sins of others. Two lines of thought found in the New Testament seem to be helpful here: the first is centred upon the phrase *for our sins*, or *for sins*, which, as the N.E.B. footnote shows, is the reading of some manuscripts. The reading of some others, *for us*, is almost certainly not original; of the other two readings—*for our sins* or simply *for sins*—it does not matter for our purpose which we choose. Either is clearly connected with the phrase 'for sin' which the reader may be surprised to find is technical; it is used in the Greek version of Lev. 5: 6 f. and Ezek. 43: 21 for what is in Hebrew 'the sin-offering' of the priestly Law. The idea behind this was apparently the felt necessity to expiate a sin; that is, as nearly as we can describe this feeling, a desire to remove the stain which the sin had brought upon the people or the land or upon both. Hebrews makes much of the argument that there was a system of sacrifices in the temple in Jerusalem which were designed 'for sin', that is to remove the stain of sin, to expiate it. Once every year, on the Day of Atonement, the high priest entered the Holy of Holies of the temple, to atone for all the sins for which no atonement had been made during the past year. Now all these sins received expiation only outwardly, as we saw when discussing 1: 16 (p. 24). Expiation for the sin within the heart, or, we might say, for the real sin itself, could be made only by one with the authority and nature of God himself, one whom God himself provided. Such expiation would not be made on a yearly

Day of Atonement but *once and for all*. This character of the offering of Christ as a high priest not of the temple but of the universe is emphasized by Paul in Rom. 6: 10 (again, 'once for all') and especially in Hebrews, nowhere more forcefully than in 9: 11–14. That whole passage should be read, but the main claim is that of verse 12: 'he has entered the sanctuary once and for all and secured an eternal deliverance.'

The other line of thought centres on the words *to bring us to God*. It was explained on page 14 when discussing 1: 1–2 that sin was regarded as a barrier between men and God. This is a real barrier to all men, and the sense of ceremonial impurity which prevented the ancient worshipper from approaching his god, but which could be removed by a mere outward rite, is only an analogy to it, a picture of it. This outward rite, as we have called it, often consisted of the slaughter of an animal. The way was then open, through this gift, to the god. Although this may seem a false notion to us, the reality of which it is a picture is not false or imaginary: we do need a way to be opened up for us through the barrier of sin. Hebrews says that by his own death Christ opened up the way. The whole passage 9: 23–8 should be read, but verse 24 sums up part of what we are meant to understand: 'Christ has entered, not that sanctuary made by men's hands which is only a symbol of the reality, but heaven itself, to appear now before God on our behalf.' 1 Peter does not mention here the idea of Christ appearing in heaven 'on our behalf' (i.e. to intercede for us) but another thought hinted at in the words *to bring us to God*. This is clearly expressed in Heb. 10: 20, 'the new, living way which he has opened for us through the curtain, the way of his flesh'. The suggestion is that we can follow Christ through union with his death and resurrection, from the sphere of this life into that of eternal life, called in the second half of this verse 3: 18, as often in the New Testament, just *life*. ✳

DIGRESSION: THE DISOBEDIENT SPIRITS
AND BAPTISM

18b In the body he was put to death; in the spirit he was
19 brought to life. And in the spirit he went and made his
20 proclamation to the imprisoned spirits. They had refused
obedience long ago, while God waited patiently in the
days of Noah and the building of the ark, and in the ark
a few persons, eight in all, were brought to safety through
21 the water. This water prefigured the water of baptism
through which you are now brought to safety. Baptism
is not the washing away of bodily pollution, but the
appeal made to God by a good conscience; and it brings
22 salvation through the resurrection of Jesus Christ, who
entered heaven after receiving the submission of angelic
authorities and powers, and is now at the right hand of
God.

✳ 18b. *In the body he was put to death; in the spirit he was
brought to life*: thus translated, these words might be taken to
mean that Jesus was first of all put to death, and then afterwards by the power of the Spirit brought to life again. This
seems to be the teaching of much of the New Testament, for
which it would be unnecessary to quote a great many passages:
1 Cor. 15: 4 will be enough: 'he was raised to life on the
third day.' Again, readers of Luke's gospel and of the first
chapter of Acts would say that there was a long period (forty
days) between the resurrection and the ascent to the throne at
the right hand of God; but elsewhere there is no such long
gap. One example will suffice: in John 20: 17 Jesus, when
speaking to Mary of Magdala, had 'not yet ascended', but
the same evening appeared to the disciples and gave them the
Holy Spirit (John 20: 23), an event which according to Luke
did not happen until after the Ascension, itself forty days after

the resurrection. Other writers, such as the author of Hebrews, know nothing of a gap in time between the death of Jesus and his entry into heaven; in 10: 12 he says, 'Christ offered for all time one sacrifice for sins, and took his seat at the right hand of God'; and other passages, some of which have been quoted in the discussion of the previous verse, suggest that it was by his death that Christ immediately entered the eternal realm. The Greek here means literally 'put to death indeed in the flesh but made to live in the spirit' and it may well be that here *the spirit* is best understood as a sphere of existence and a level of life beyond this. Of this sphere of existence we know nothing and such hints as we have of it are expressed in obvious picture language, such as that which speaks of Christ seated on a throne at the right hand of God. We are now in a position to understand the next verse, one of the most interesting in the New Testament.

19. If we accept the idea of the spirit as a sphere of existence there is no need to try to examine where *the imprisoned spirits* are. Nothing is said here, for example, about their being under the earth. Where is left unexplained. (Eph. 4: 9, according to one interpretation, does imagine Christ as descending 'to the regions beneath the earth' (N.E.B. footnote) but not as preaching there.) When we ask who were *the imprisoned spirits* the most natural answer, based on what would be in the mind of an author of this period, would be the 'fallen angels' of the Book of Jubilees 5 (based on Gen. 6: 1–8) and the Book of Enoch 6. These books were written at a time not exactly known, but not long before 100 B.C. In I Enoch 10: 11–14 these disobedient spirits are imprisoned in an abyss and await the judgement. We meet the idea again in Jude 6, a book whose author certainly knew I Enoch, and in 2 Pet. 2: 4. Again, in I Enoch 12: 1–4 Enoch is mysteriously hidden and is then sent to the imprisoned spirits to proclaim to them their fate, his journey taking up a large part of the following section of the book. Noah in Genesis and in Jubilees (which is a kind of rewritten Genesis) is

contrasted with these 'fallen angels' or *disobedient spirits*. The tradition that he was righteous (Gen. 6: 9) reappears in Heb. 11: 7. This seems therefore the most natural answer to the problem of the identification of these spirits; but if the next verse seems to imply that they include the departed shades of men and women who had lived on earth at the time of Noah, it may be that the author is thinking of them also, and of them as representative of the wicked among mankind, for those of the generation of Noah were regarded as a specially wicked generation on the strength of the account in Genesis. Perhaps the author is like other human beings in vaguely classing together spirit beings, who have never lived a human life but are thought to exist in some shadowy realm, and the departed spirits of human beings. Many have thought this, and thought that here we have a picture of Christ going to preach to all the departed who had lived before his time on earth and had therefore had no opportunity to hear the gospel and to repent. They therefore imagine him as making his way between Good Friday and Easter Day through Hell, a vaguely grim place below the earth, preaching to the 'lost', those imagined as being denied heaven through not knowing the gospel or refusing it; this is the medieval 'Harrowing of Hell'. It can only be said that there is no mention either of all these people or of hell in the actual passage of 1 Peter here, though 4: 6 implies that Jesus preached to the dead in this way. What is clear is that the author imagined that Jesus, made alive in the spirit, made *his proclamation to the imprisoned spirits*, and after 'receiving' their 'submission', 'took his seat' (Heb. 10: 12) 'at the right hand of God' (see verse 22 below, with the comment upon it).

20–1. The connexion of the disobedient spirits with the *days of Noah* brings in the themes of the destruction of the world by water and the saving of those who are baptized through water. The association of thought between these themes is not obvious but can be made clear: the disobedience of the spirits was the cause of the sin of the world, and led to

The Calling of a Christian

I PETER 3: 18–22

its destruction. Through the water of destruction only *a few persons, eight in all, were brought to safety*. This was by means of the ark built, according to I Enoch 67:2, by angels. Just as the eight in Noah's ark passed through the waters to physical *safety*, so the baptized pass through to spiritual *safety*. Noah's group was only eight. Those baptized into the name of Jesus can be numberless. The water of baptism, passing through which brings spiritual *safety*, is unexpectedly compared to the water of the great Flood which provided an ordeal through which the eight had to pass, and which was the death of the unworthy. That water represented the forces of chaos which God normally held in check. When the Christian goes down into the water of his baptism he not only loses his sinful life but he is committed to a fight with the forces of chaos, represented in his day by the hostile forces of political powers (thought to be given their force by spiritual 'powers') which may bring about his death. At the same time this water of baptism is that through which he must pass to *safety*. It is because of the double quality of water, as saving in a spiritual sense but reminding of the hostile forces in another, that the destructive water of the Flood *prefigured the water of baptism through which you are now brought to safety*. If some such explanation as this is not provided, we must accuse our author of a strange idea of prefigurement, for the water of the Flood destroyed while that of baptism saves.

It seems as though the author realizes that his readers may be surprised by the ideas he has just put forward, and that they may think of baptism in the way explained in the note on 1: 15–16 (p. 24), believing that sin caused both a spiritual pollution which must be counteracted by repentance, and a kind of *bodily pollution* which needed a ceremonial cleansing; he therefore goes on to say what he thinks baptism to be, first saying quite firmly that it *is not the washing away of bodily pollution*.

When we come to decide what the author wishes to say baptism is (in contrast to what it is not) we meet a difficulty,

53

because the words used are highly technical. Before we attempt an explanation, it may be well to remark that the one given here is longer than any given elsewhere in this commentary, and to give the reason for this. No such long explanations are offered in other passages because this would seem to base the commentary on the Greek text rather than on the N.E.B. and would make it very complicated; but not giving these explanations does give the impression that the expressions and vocabulary are throughout simpler than they really are in the Greek, which is an educated and sophisticated Greek. This, incidentally, is really a very strong reason for rejecting the view that Peter himself wrote the work.

In its translation, *the appeal made to God by a good conscience*, the N.E.B. does not make clear what *the appeal* is for. In the Greek version of Dan. 4: 14, the word (*eperotema*) here translated 'appeal' means 'judgement' or 'decision', which would make sense if applied here: 'the decision of a good conscience (to turn) towards God'. But in the Greek Old Testament the usual meaning is rather 'inquiry', that is inquiry of God, seeking an answer as a pagan might of a divine oracle. So in 1 Sam. 9: 9 to inquire of God clearly means asking for an answer, through some quasi-magical or supernatural means, to a problem (e.g. as in this story in 1 Sam. 9, which could be reduced to such words as 'What has happened to my lost donkeys?'). Ecclus. 33: 3 uses this idea in a skilful way to express a man not merely inquiring of but regulating his whole life by the Law (read the whole passage 32: 23 — 33: 3). An extension of this meaning 'inquiry' is 'request' or 'demand'. The verb is common in the synoptic gospels in both these senses, although the noun occurs only here in the New Testament. A possible translation is therefore 'a request to God for a good conscience', and this makes good sense because it says what baptism is, clearly parallel to what it is not, in the first part of the assertion. But baptism would seem to be more than just a request, and a meaning which would illuminate the whole ceremony, in which it seems that there was not only a washing but also a demand made and an assurance given, would obviously seem appropriate. We must therefore consider a possibility which arises from the use of the word in contemporary papyri. Here the Greek *eperotema* is the equivalent of the Latin *stipulatio*, and was the name for a clause in a business contract taking its name from one of its two parts, the formal *eperotema* or stipulation, i.e. demand made by one of the contracting parties, and the consent (Greek, *homologia*) of the other party. Now if the meaning is to be understood against this background and the word is taken to mean 'demand', baptism may be said here to be a request or appeal, just as was decided on other grounds already. But if the word means the whole formality of demand and consent together, we may wonder if the author has in mind the sort of scene sketched in Acts 8: 37, a verse to be found only in some manuscripts of Acts and certainly not to be ascribed to the original, but added early enough to show what was usual in a baptism in the early church. Here the eunuch meets Philip's demand, 'If you whole-heartedly believe, it is permitted', with the words, 'I believe Jesus Christ is the Son of God', which is his assent or 'confession' (not in the sense we use when we speak of a 'confession' of being wrong but of a formal profession of one's belief, the very thing which in Greek is called *homologia*). The word translated *conscience* is not quite what we mean by the word (though that would be difficult to define, in any case); it means something more like a disposition of the mind, including the meaning of conscience as the sense of right and wrong, but not confined to it. If then *eperotema* refers to the whole formality of contract-making and applies it to Christian baptism, the translation offered by one scholar, 'the assurance before God of a loyal attitude of mind', may be accepted, though with the understanding that the full meaning is something like 'the assurance, in response to formal demand, of a loyal attitude of mind towards God'. This would have the advantage of contrasting the Christian, who throughout the work is summoned to obedience even, or perhaps chiefly, in face of hardship, with the disobedient spirits of verses 19 and 20 above.

21. *it brings salvation through the resurrection of Jesus Christ* because it is *not* a mere *washing*, but, as well as what it has been affirmed to be in the previous sentence, a uniting of the Christian (if he really believes) with Christ in his resurrection, as we have already seen (p. 39, note on 2: 24).

22. For the meaning of the symbolic phrase, *the right hand of God*, see the note on verse 18 above (p. 49). *The submission of angelic authorities and powers* concisely summarizes a very important idea in the New Testament. Every day men met forces with which they had to reckon. Some of these were friendly, some were partly hostile, some wholly hostile. All were under God's authority, those hostile to men being permitted rather than deliberately authorized by him. These forces were personified in men's minds and were thought to inhabit spheres above the earth whence they influenced the course of events below. Behind each political power, for instance, there stood one of these spiritual 'authorities' or 'powers', not wholly obedient to God's will. In Rom. 13: 1 ff. Paul teaches that the earthly power, in the sense of a political authority, must be obeyed, no doubt because he believed the spiritual power behind it was subservient to God. Satan was a supreme example of such a 'power'—the chief of the 'powers' hostile to men—and in Luke 4: 6 he claims that all the kingdoms of the world make up a 'dominion' which 'has been put in my hands'. The early Christians believed that this was how the universe was governed and that by his obedient death Christ had won a place over all and received *the submission of angelic authorities and powers*. In this way Ps. 110: 1 was fulfilled, 'The Lord saith unto my lord, Sit thou at my right hand, Until I make thine enemies thy footstool'. Here 'my lord' is thought to be the Messiah or Christ, and the enemies are the 'angelic powers'. *

NEW LIFE IN CHRIST

Remembering that Christ endured bodily suffering, you **4** must arm yourselves with a temper of mind like his. When a man has thus endured bodily suffering he has finished with sin, and for the rest of his days on earth he ₂ may live, not for the things that men desire, but for what God wills. You had time enough in the past to do all ₃ the things that men want to do in the pagan world. Then you lived in licence and debauchery, drunkenness, riot, and tippling, and the forbidden worship of idols. Now, ₄ when you no longer plunge with them into all this reckless dissipation, they cannot understand it, and they vilify you accordingly; but they shall answer for it to him ₅ who stands ready to pass judgement on the living and the dead. Why was the Gospel preached to those who are ₆ dead? In order that, although in the body they received the sentence common to men, they might in the spirit be alive with the life of God.

The end of all things is upon us, so you must lead an ₇ ordered and sober life, given to prayer. Above all, keep ₈ your love for one another at full strength, because love cancels innumerable sins. Be hospitable to one another ₉ without complaining. Whatever gift each of you may ₁₀ have received, use it in service to one another, like good stewards dispensing the grace of God in its varied forms. Are you a speaker? Speak as if you uttered oracles of God. ₁₁ Do you give service? Give it as in the strength which God supplies. In all things so act that the glory may be God's through Jesus Christ; to him belong glory and power for ever and ever. Amen.

1–2. We have regarded 3: 18b–22 as something of a digression about what Christ did when he died. Indeed the passage seems to be an inserted comment on a piece of teaching which was standard in the church, and had been so at least since the time of Paul. We saw 18a, 'Christ also died for our sins once and for all', to be like Rom. 6: 10. Here in 4: 1 there seems to be a continuation of that thought, found in Rom. 6: 10–11, which says in words which sum up important teaching in a remarkably concise way, 'For in dying as he died, he died to sin, once for all, and in living as he lives, he lives to God. In the same way you must regard yourselves as dead to sin and alive to God, in union with Christ Jesus.' This passage in 1 Peter is parallel to the second of Paul's sentences, and the author uses a metaphor, *arm yourselves*, like that used by Paul in Rom. 6: 13, though unfortunately the N.E.B. does not there preserve it; the Greek has 'Do not present your limbs as arms...'. It is interesting to see how the two teachers tackle the great question which arises in every attentive reader's mind, 'Granted that Christ died once and for all for our sins, *how* does that bring us to God?' Paul recognizes the likelihood of the question because he raises it himself in an acute and disturbing way, 'Shall we persist in sin, so that there may be all the more grace?' (Rom. 6: 1), and answers from the depths of his own feeling founded on conviction, 'No, no! We died to sin: how can we live in it any longer?' 1 Peter says simply, *When a man has thus endured bodily suffering he has finished with sin*... What does he mean? Perhaps he means that the Christian must regard his baptism as 'enduring bodily suffering'; this may sound strange but it is possible that baptism was regarded as an entrance into the sufferings of Christ, since it was certainly regarded, as we have seen, as an entrance into his death. Once again there is a parallel in Paul's Rom. 6. There in verse 7 he argues, 'a dead man is no longer answerable for his sin'. It is not stranger to regard a man as having 'suffered' by baptism than as having died by it; and we have seen that in 3: 21 the author was probably thinking of baptism as partly representative of an ordeal through which the Christian must pass to his salvation or 'safety'. But this cannot be the whole explanation in a work which makes one of its chief themes the patient endurance of suffering in everyday life. In fact, the meaning seems plain: baptism commits the baptized by powerful symbolism into suffering in union with Christ. This suffering may come to him in everyday life at the hands of persecutors and be, like that of his master, undeserved. He is not to curse at it or its agents, but *with a temper of mind* like that of Jesus and gained from this union, *live, not for the things which men desire, but for what God wills*. Some may say that this is impossible to accept without the eschatological hope (the hope that Christ himself would soon come to save them) but others have accepted this change in life and its aims as a direct result of their union with Christ, even though the hope is deferred.

3–6. The contrast with the old life *in the pagan world* is here clearly drawn and reads familiarly enough to modern ears, except perhaps for the *worship of idols*. Many might think that this was nothing to do with the conduct of life, since worship is in a department by itself. This illustrates the ignorance which prevails about pagan religion: it was not moral nor even morally neutral, but encouraged as part of its exercise sometimes both drunkenness and sexual vice and laxity. Philosophers, Jews and Christians provided by both teaching and example a strong contrast with this prevailing laxity which was closely connected with worship. Religion is not necessarily good: it needs to be true and to make demands for a moral life before it can be commended.

The words *they cannot understand it* reveal much; they are true for the time when they were written, for as we have seen (p. 34 on 2: 12) fantastic scandals were widespread about Christians, who were taken to be criminals. It did not occur to the average pagan, even if he was well educated, that any group of people would meet secretly in order to promote purity and goodness of life. We may imagine that they would always look for a selfish motive. Modern pagans echo the lack of understanding, asking cynically, 'What do they get out of it? Don't tell me they do it for the love of it!' *They vilify* Christians *accordingly*.

5–6. *him who stands ready to pass judgement on the living and the dead* probably means Christ, to whom it was believed that God had committed the final *judgement*. The clearest picture is given by Paul: 1 Thess. 4: 13–18 and 1 Cor. 15: 51–7 both show that he expected the judgement to be carried out first on the dead, who would be raised to life for this purpose, and then on the living. The latter are in old-fashioned English sometimes called 'the quick', so the Creed speaks of Christ's coming 'to judge both the quick and the dead'. When writing to the Thessalonians, Paul had to answer their anxious question as to what would happen to the Christians who had died before Christ's coming. His answer was that they would be raised from the dead to meet him. It is easy to imagine that the question which would develop later would be, 'What would be the fate at the judgement of those who had never heard the gospel?' In verse 6 this is answered by the implication that the gospel was preached to them. The words *in the spirit be alive with the life of God* recall 3: 18 *b*, 'in the spirit he was brought to life', where Christ is the subject and a passage follows to the effect that he went and preached after his death to 'the imprisoned spirits'. From the present passage it seems that the earlier one meant to imply that Christ preached to all the dead, although there was no clear hint there that this was the meaning. Notice once again how *alive with the life of God* recalls Paul in Rom. 6: 11, 'alive to God'. If the dead thereby heard the gospel they could at the final judgement be judged by whether they accepted it or not. This is not the same solution as that of Paul, which may be nearer to that which would be acceptable to us. He argues in Rom. 10: 18 ff. that the gospel had already been preached 'all over the earth', apparently by the prophets; and

he states that 'Gentiles, who made no effort after righteousness, nevertheless achieved it' (Rom. 9: 30). Thus he appears
to mean that men may be judged by their response to something which can be taken as equivalent to the gospel in that it
was a challenge from God in their own day.

7–11. The commentary in this series on Jas. 5: 8 draws
attention to the parallel here and in Phil. 4: 6, 'The Lord is
near', and refers to the discussion in 2 Pet. 3: 1–14 where the
imminent *end of all things* is made the reason for sobriety and
prayer. The commentator approves of the answer given to
mockers in 2 Pet. 3: 8, but see also the comment on that
passage in this book. It is better not to emphasize the argument,
which can easily be misrepresented: on the one hand the
Christian is urged to count himself 'happy' (1 Pet. 3: 14) if he
suffers for doing good, and it is implied that this is a way of
fellowship with Christ; but we have already seen that this
apparently high ethic was demanded because it was believed
that the Christian could expect an early vindication. This may
appear to detract from the high ethical tone; but those who
wrote these things often faced martyr deaths without having
been vindicated in the way they had hoped. Indeed, 2 Peter
is concerned with this very problem; but we must not overlook the power by which Christians became martyrs without
the consolation they had looked for; their actions were even
better than their words. It is not quite clear what is meant by
love cancels innumerable sins; those of the one who gives or of
the one who receives the love? It cannot be a reference simply
to the love of God in cancelling the sins of men, though the
word *cancels* (literally, in the Greek, 'covers'), no doubt
represents the Hebrew word for 'cover', which has a meaning
usually represented in English by 'atone for', since it is used
of certain sacrifices in the Old Testament. 'Blessed is he whose
transgression is forgiven, whose sin is covered', says Ps. 32: 1.
When Prov. 10: 12 says, 'Hatred stirreth up strifes; But love
covereth all transgressions', the original meaning may have
been obvious and simple, but it could be taken to mean that

love covered in the sense of expiating, wiping out and taking out of existence all transgressions. It is possible that this verse in Proverbs was the model for the saying in Jas. 5: 20, 'Any man who brings a sinner back from his crooked ways will be rescuing his soul from death and cancelling innumerable sins', and for the saying here in I Peter. Perhaps the kind of love which the writer had in mind was that which brought back a sinner from his wicked ways, so that the sins cancelled are those of the one who receives the love, love which must be of the quality described in I Cor. 13: 7, love which has 'no limit to its faith, its hope, and its endurance'. In that case it has a kind of atoning force, because it may win back a lapsing Christian to the love of God who alone forgives sins.

In a situation where there were as yet no churches built and the Christians were a persecuted minority, *hospitality* was an essential part of the Christian life, particularly in providing places for meeting and for the visiting ministry of prophets, evangelists and teachers, as well as of apostles in the earliest days. The practice is reflected in many places in the New Testament, Paul often having occasion to thank the members of his churches for their generosity in this way and to request them to give hospitality to his fellow-workers when he sent them to different places. He too commends it as a virtue necessary for the church's life in Rom. 12: 13, the whole passage here being paralleled by Rom. 12: 6 ff., I Cor. 12: 4 ff. and Eph. 4: 7. All these teach the main point made here, which is apt to be missed by the cursory reader: all ability, even such as would give a man an authoritative position in the church, must be seen as one of the gifts of God to his church. This is specially clear in Rom. 12: 8, where the leader is apparently regarded as having just one gift among many distributed by the Spirit to the different members of the church; in the same way here both the *speaker* and he who can *give service* (the latter being signified by a verb which suggests a servant) are to regard what they can do as done *in the strength which God supplies*. This main portion of the work now ends with a doxology or ascription of praise to God, suggesting that it was originally a sermon, if not a whole liturgy, as explained on p. 15. ✳

THE ATTACHED LETTER

✳ The remaining part of the work is more easily recognizable as a letter: the persecution mentioned is already upon the readers. It is official, and no longer only a possibility or a matter of daily petty persecution from neighbour or master. A direct appeal is made to 'suffer as a Christian', and an even more direct one to be awake and 'on the alert' because 'the time has come for the judgement to begin'. ✳

MEETING PERSECUTION

My dear friends, do not be bewildered by the fiery 12 ordeal that is upon you, as though it were something extraordinary. It gives you a share in Christ's sufferings, 13 and that is cause for joy; and when his glory is revealed, your joy will be triumphant. If Christ's name is flung in 14 your teeth as an insult, count yourselves happy, because then that glorious Spirit which is the Spirit of God is resting upon you. If you suffer, it must not be for 15 murder, theft, or sorcery, nor for infringing the rights of others. But if anyone suffers as a Christian, he should 16 feel it no disgrace, but confess that name to the honour of God.

The time has come for the judgement to begin; it is 17 beginning with God's own household. And if it is starting with you, how will it end for those who refuse to obey the gospel of God? And if it is hard enough for the 18 righteous to be saved, what will become of the impious

19 and sinful? So even those who suffer, if it be according to God's will, should commit their souls to him—by doing good; their Maker will not fail them.

✻ *12–16. The fiery ordeal that is upon you* seems to suggest that the writer is now addressing friends undergoing an actual organized persecution. This is different from, for example, the situation in which the author can hope that no harm will happen to them if they do good, but that they may have to suffer for their virtues, as in 3: 13. They are not to *be bewildered* by it, not only because suffering may be the lot of a Christian in everyday life, but because it is to be expected in God's plan. It is not obvious here, but the heavy emphasis from this point onwards on the end having arrived shows that the *share in Christ's sufferings* means more than facing suffering in the same spirit as Christ (4: 1). It means here sharing in the Messianic woes, that is, the woes that are to come upon the earth, according to early Christian belief, just before the return of the Messiah or Christ. They are the subject of the 'Little Apocalypse' in Mark 13: 5–37 and parallels. In Mark, Jesus warns his disciples, 'All will hate you for your allegiance to me; but the man who holds out to the end will be saved' (13: 13), and declares that if God 'had not cut short that time of troubles, no living thing could survive' (13: 20). Earlier, these times have been described as 'the birth-pangs of the new age' (13: 8) and towards the end of the whole discourse Jesus says, 'Be alert, be wakeful' (13: 33). Although the time of the end of these days of trouble cannot be known, 'after that distress' (13: 24) there will be signs in the universe and 'Then they will see the Son of Man coming in the clouds with great power and glory' (13: 26). Our author refers to these times, and reminds his readers that a share in these sufferings *is cause for joy*, because *when his glory is revealed, your joy will be triumphant*.

Suffering for *Christ's name* (verse 14) or *as a Christian* (verse 16) reflects a persecution in which it is an offence simply to be

64

a Christian and not to renounce the name if challenged. The situation seems to be of the kind described in Pliny's Letter to Trajan given on p. 9. Since 1 Peter is written to regions which include Pliny's province of Bithynia-Pontus, it is a reasonable view to hold that the letter is addressed to that very situation. The term *Christian* seems to have been given originally to those of mixed race, Jews and Gentiles, who believed and proclaimed that the Christ (Messiah) had come and was to be awaited in an early return. Luke tells us that the term was first used in Antioch (Acts 11: 26). When Agrippa (Acts 26: 28) resisted Paul's argument, implying that it would take more to 'make a Christian of' him, he probably reflected the popular distaste for the word and the people it was used to designate. Tacitus, in the passage mentioned on p. 34, seems to imply that the word meant to most people somebody bad, for he speaks of 'a class hated for their abominations, called Christians by the populace'. This adds point to the words in verse 16, *he should feel it no disgrace, but confess that name to the honour of God.* Two further points remain which arise out of verse 14: the first is the word *happy*, so close to the word *insult*. The Greek recalls clearly Matt. 5: 11, 'How blest you are, when you suffer insults and persecution...for my sake'. The second is that while the language about *the Spirit of God...resting upon* Christians when they are persecuted for the name of Christ may derive from Isa. 61: 1, the thought here is like that of Mark 13: 11 which instructs the disciples that they are not to worry beforehand about their defence 'for it will not be you that speak, but the Holy Spirit'. In the discussion of 3: 15 ('Be always ready with your defence') it seemed as though there was a contradiction. This may be removed if we imagine that the teaching there was for every day, and that in Mark 13: 11 it is for a time when the Christian is actually arrested and taken for trial.

Of course we are not to imagine that the writer thinks a Christian is likely to *suffer...for murder* or any other crime. He is rather making the point that while, as everyone would admit, it would be a *disgrace* to be punished for such crimes, it would not be a *disgrace* but an honour to suffer for Christ's name.

infringing the rights of others is a reasonable guess at the meaning of a word found only here and once elsewhere in later Christian literature. It may well be a colloquial term of the period, but it has not turned up in any papyrus so far.

17–19. It is very important to see that the author thinks that the times in which he and his readers are living are the beginning of the end of the age, a view shared with all the writers in the New Testament. The particular point made here is interesting: he interprets the persecution of which he speaks as the beginning of *the judgement*, that is, God's judgement. It follows that in his view the unjust actions of civil rulers could be regarded as God at work in the world. He seems also to believe that there is an ordeal in store for everyone, of special severity for sinners, for he asks, *if it is hard enough for the righteous to be saved, what will become of the impious and sinful?* He identifies the latter with *those who refuse to obey the gospel of God.* If the Christians who suffer *commit their souls to* God they will follow Jesus himself, who said, according to Luke 23: 46 (in Luke alone): 'Father, into thy hands I commend my spirit.' As 1 Peter said in 2: 23, he 'committed his cause to the One who judges justly'.

19. *by doing good* seems to envisage further life on this earth, and reminds us of 2: 15 where 'by your good conduct you should put ignorance and stupidity to silence'. Many argue that because of this there is here no reference to persecution by the state; but the problem is not that the persecution envisaged seems by these words to be at the hands of neighbours, but that in the midst of a passage affirming the early end of the age everyday *doing good* seems to be commended.

20. Since God is *their maker* they may trust him to give them new life; this is the conviction on which the Christian hope of eternal life is based. ✻

STAND FAST!

And now I appeal to the elders of your community, as a 5
fellow-elder and a witness of Christ's sufferings, and also
a partaker in the splendour that is to be revealed. Tend 2
that flock of God whose shepherds you are, and do it,
not under compulsion, but of your own free will, as God
would have it; not for gain but out of sheer devotion;
not tyrannizing over those who are allotted to your care, 3
but setting an example to the flock. And then, when the 4
Head Shepherd appears, you will receive for your own
the unfading garland of glory.

In the same way you younger men must be subordinate 5
to your elders. Indeed, all of you should wrap yourselves
in the garment of humility towards each other, because
God sets his face against the arrogant but favours the
humble. Humble yourselves then under God's mighty 6
hand, and he will lift you up in due time. Cast all your 7
cares on him, for you are his charge.

Awake! be on the alert! Your enemy the devil, like 8
a roaring lion, prowls round looking for someone to
devour. Stand up to him, firm in faith, and remember 9
that your brother Christians are going through the same
kinds of suffering while they are in the world. And the 10
God of all grace, who called you into his eternal glory in
Christ, will himself, after your brief suffering, restore,
establish, and strengthen you on a firm foundation. He 11
holds dominion for ever and ever. Amen.

* 1–4. This appeal to the *elders* of a church undergoing
persecution is no mere formality. It was quite common in the
early church to find men refusing to accept office in it out of

modesty; in time of danger apparent modesty might well mask fear of responsibility. Those who were already elders would therefore act, especially in relation to secular officials, *under compulsion* unless they remembered that they held their position in the *flock of God* and must act not from any ordinary principle or motive, but *as God would have it*. The language here is paralleled by the speech of Paul at Miletus as given in Acts 20: 18–35, which was reviewed in the note on 2: 25 (p. 40). There too the elders are called 'shepherds of the church of the Lord' (Acts 20: 28) and are warned against 'savage wolves', though in that context it seems that the wolves would be false teachers rather than persecutors. Here no enemies are mentioned, but the whole passage implies that the church is beginning to pass through its final ordeal. The writer does not lose sight of the fact that there may be some periods of relative peace when office might be accepted for the sake of the money subscribed by the members of the church for their officers. This is an inducement hard to imagine in modern times, but was evidently a real danger in the period following the apostles, for we find evidence of it in the Pastoral Letters. 1 Tim. 3: 3 insists in a way which surprises the modern reader that the bishop must not be a 'lover of money', and Titus 1: 7 uses the same expression as here, *for gain* (there 'money-grubber', an adjective), as something to be avoided in a bishop.

Elders were the natural officers for people with a Jewish background to appoint in a church, and Paul and Barnabas are reported to have appointed them 'in each congregation' on their missionary journey (Acts 14: 23). So natural was this that Luke makes even the church at Jerusalem, usually thought of as that of the apostles, and therefore of a different and more authoritative kind than any other church (a character which it has in the eyes of as late a churchman as Eusebius, in the first years of the fourth century), a church of 'apostles and elders' (Acts 15: 4, 6, 22, 23). This spirit is reflected when the writer, calling himself 'Peter, apostle' at the very beginning of the Letter, calls himself here *a fellow-elder*, thus showing humble fellowship with his readers; it cannot be a slip on the part of the real author who thus reveals that he is no more than an elder, for he goes on to claim to be *a witness of Christ's sufferings* and so is evidently conscious of his adopted role as Peter. We may be tempted to ask how far this might be true of the real Peter, since 'the disciples all deserted' Jesus 'and ran away' (Mark 14: 50); Peter had remained at a distance when Jesus was tried in the high priest's house, and the only followers of Jesus present at the crucifixion were 'a number of women', 'watching from a distance', according to Mark 15: 40. The account in John 19: 25–30 is quite inconsistent with this, and is of more than doubtful historicity, and in any case does not include Peter as present at the crucifixion. It is unnecessary to do more than remind ourselves of these facts, because *a witness* in this sense includes the sense of martyr, the word being the same in Greek. It seems therefore certain that there is a reference here to Peter as a martyr for Christ. The facts were reviewed in the note on 1: 1 (p. 3); it is interesting that in 1 Clement 5: 4 Peter is spoken of as one who 'after thus witnessing went to the place of glory which was his due'. This reflects the same thought as here, where the martyr is also *a partaker in the splendour that is to be revealed*.

For Christ himself as *the Head Shepherd* (though the exact word—one only in Greek—occurs only here in the New Testament) see the note on 2: 25 (p. 40).

4. *the unfading garland of glory* or a very similar expression occurs often in the Bible to signify an intangible reward from God, and occurs twice in the Dead Sea Scrolls. According to Rev. 2: 10, the risen Jesus promises 'the crown of life' and Paul in 2 Tim. 4: 8 confidently expects after death 'the garland of righteousness'. It contrasts with the 'fading wreath' (1 Cor. 9: 25) which was the prize of the athlete, and it means eternal life.

5–7. That *younger men* should *be subordinate to* their *elders* was a strict rule at Qumran, and according to Josephus, also among the Essenes, a strict ascetic sect of the Jews at this time. This injunction is natural in any community, but here and in other communities of Jewish ancestry it is made a religious duty. *Elders* here means simply the older men, but they would be largely the same, at any rate in a small church, as the elders in a technical sense. This exhortation to *humility* is like Jas. 4: 6 which also quotes *God sets his face against the arrogant but favours the humble* from Prov. 3: 34. The *due time* at which God will *lift up* the humble is the day of judgement, 'when the Head Shepherd appears' (verse 4). It is not merely a matter of being humble so that this position can be reversed later; this would merely be priggish. The writer has in mind the ordeal his readers are now undergoing, and, consistently with the lofty but difficult teaching of the whole work, urges them to *humble* themselves *under God's mighty hand* so as to pass through the test.

8–11. Sometimes in the Bible a scene is imagined in heaven, or in the presence of God, at which the destiny of men and nations is decided, and which takes the form of a court of justice. In this court God is judge, and the prosecutor, accuser or slanderer (the meaning of the Greek word which has given us the English *devil*) is an evil angel, the evil angel *par excellence*, the *enemy* (just as Satan is Hebrew for adversary). Israel's protector angel is Michael, who appears as such in Dan. 10: 13 and 12: 1. We find Michael 'in debate with the devil' in Jude 9, and in Rev. 12: 7–9 at war with him. All this happens 'in heaven', behind the scenes of this world; but when persecution breaks out, the power of Satan or the devil is felt in this world. Indeed, the political situation had so often been like this that the prevalent belief was that the devil had dominion over this world, allowed him by God temporarily, a dominion disputed by Jesus. In Luke 4: 6 the devil claims, 'All this dominion...has been put in my hands.' When in a persecution accusers were abroad looking for Christians whom they might accuse before the Roman authorities it was natural to say *the devil...prowls round looking for someone to devour.* The use of words like *a roaring lion* may reveal quite a scholarly knowledge of scripture; the Targum (Aramaic version) of the prophets frequently interprets the word 'lion' by a king, who is either explicitly or by implication hostile. It is therefore appropriate to compare the devil, hostile king of this world, to a lion. Our interpretation of the whole passage is supported by the fact that the word here rendered *enemy* means literally an adversary in a law-court.

Stand up to him is very like Jas. 4: 7, 'Stand up to the devil and he will turn and run', and the call to 'stand your ground' and 'stand firm' in Eph. 6: 13-14. The trials to which the devil may submit Christians are various, but this passage suggests that the basic teaching on resistance to the devil, perhaps regularly given at baptism, was connected with the danger of persecution to which they were liable by entering the church. If there is a reference to this teaching here, it gives point to the injunction to remember that *brother Christians* are destined for the same sort of suffering so long as *they are in the world.* The world contrasts with the eternal sphere into which Christians have entered already (God *called you into his eternal glory*) but which has yet to be revealed as the new order to take the place of the old. God *holds dominion for ever and ever*, in contrast to the devil whose dominion is of this world and for this age alone. ✳

FINAL GREETINGS

I write you this brief appeal through Silvanus, our trusty 12
brother as I hold him, adding my testimony that this is
the true grace of God. In this stand fast.

Greetings from her who dwells in Babylon, chosen by 13
God like you, and from my son Mark. Greet one another 14
with the kiss of love.

Peace to you all who belong to Christ!

✳ 12. *I write you this brief appeal through Silvanus:* if Peter really wrote the letter the interpretation explained in the note on 1: 1 (p. 7), according to which Silvanus is Silas the companion of Paul, holds good. If the work is pseudonymous and, as we have seen to be probable, of the early second century, it seems unlikely from the wording of this verse that the Silvanus here mentioned is the actual author of the letter. It seems therefore to many that the use of his name is part of the pseudonymous device; but in that case there is here a real attempt to deceive, to obtain authority for the work which would not otherwise have been conceded. If this would not at the time have been thought reprehensible, it still seems a lame device, since the date of the work would preclude the recipients from thinking that Peter himself, who died about A.D. 64, could really be writing to them. We are forced to the conclusion that while the real author remains unknown he was referring to a real Silvanus, but one otherwise unknown to us.

13. Very early manuscripts added a word which would make it necessary to translate 'Greetings from the church who dwells in Babylon...'. This shows that it was early assumed that this was the meaning, as indeed it probably is. This, and the other possible interpretation, are explained in the commentary on 1: 1 (p. 4). If the writer meant his wife, *my son Mark* is natural and requires no explanation, except that it does not necessarily mean the Mark of Acts and can refer to the son of the unknown author; for Mark was a very common name. If Peter is the author, Mark may well be the Mark of Acts to whose mother's home Peter went after escaping from prison (Acts 12: 12) and who accompanied Paul and Barnabas from Jerusalem to Cyprus (Acts 12: 25; 13: 6) and who left them at that point (13: 13) to Paul's disgust (15: 38). He accompanied Barnabas again to Cyprus (15: 39) and seems to have regained Paul's favour later on (Col. 4: 10 and 2 Tim. 4: 11). The last reference may suggest that he came to Rome to help Paul at the end, so he might well have been also Peter's assistant in Rome, if this letter was written by Peter

himself. Papias, as already explained on p. 11, says just this of him.

14. *the kiss of love* almost certainly refers to the greeting given at the eucharist, at which this work would be read. The kiss was a normal greeting between man and man as well as between woman and woman. This is clear from such passages as Luke 7: 45 where Jesus reproaches his host for giving him no kiss (in that passage the woman's kissing Jesus's feet is exceptional and shows her deep feeling of humility) and from the famous kiss of Judas (Mark 14: 45 and parallel passages). Its use in the Eucharist is probably the explanation of the occurrences in Paul's letters, e.g. 1 Cor. 16: 20, and is testified by Justin's *Apology* 1: 65 (c. 160). At first an actual kiss, it became later formalized into a bow with the hands upon the other's shoulders.

Peace to you all: this form of final greeting is unique although we find 'joy and peace' in Rom. 15: 13, which may have been intended originally for an ending. The word usually used by Paul and in letters imitating his is 'grace'. The salutation here may be connected with the kiss referred to in the last note, which was later called the Kiss of Peace. Thus Hippolytus of Rome gives a description of the Eucharist at Rome about 225 which includes the following: 'And when the catechumens finish their prayers, they must not give the kiss of peace, for their kiss is not yet pure. Only believers shall salute one another, but men with men and women with women; a man shall not salute a woman.' (Catechumens are those being intructed for baptism.)

✳   ✳   ✳   ✳   ✳   ✳   ✳   ✳   ✳   ✳   ✳   ✳   ✳

A LETTER OF JUDE
THE SECOND LETTER OF PETER

A LETTER OF
JUDE

THE SECOND LETTER OF
PETER

✻ ✻ ✻ ✻ ✻ ✻ ✻ ✻ ✻ ✻ ✻ ✻ ✻

STRUCTURE

A Letter of Jude and the Second Letter of Peter have so much in common that it is clear either that one used the other or that both derive from a common source. Jude is much shorter than 2 Peter, and so much of it is found in 2 Peter (especially in 2 Pet. 2: 1–22) that if we tried to reconstruct any common source we should find it very nearly identical with Jude. For that reason the common source theory is less likely to be the right explanation of the likeness between them; it is more probable either that 2 Peter used Jude or that Jude use 2 Peter.

There can be no certainty as to which of these is right, but the most natural explanation seems to be that Jude was written first and then 2 Peter expanded it. One general consideration can be put forward at once, and then some passages of the two letters may be compared; the general consideration is that if 2 Peter was the first to be written, Jude must have extracted the middle (2 Pet. 2: 1–22) and taken this as his basis, using one or two verses from elsewhere in 2 Peter, but neglected the rest. This is not impossible, but it is less likely than that 2 Peter expanded Jude by the addition of further material, thus making Jude the main part of a new

Letter. We may now compare some passages of the two letters; the first is a comparison of the two lists of God's judgements in the past:

Jude 6–7, 11	2 Pet. 2: 4–6, 15
Disobedient Israelites	[Disobedient Israelites
Fallen Angels	omitted]
[Flood omitted]	Fallen Angels
Sodom and Gomorrah	Flood
Cain, Balaam, Korah	Sodom and Gomorrah
[in wrong time order]	Balaam
	[in right time order]

Again we cannot be certain, but it seems unlikely that Jude would alter 2 Peter by making a list in the wrong chronological order and above all omit the Flood. 2 Peter might well drop the disobedient Israelites because they were in the wrong order and might well add the famous Flood, keeping all in the correct chronological order. In each case of a judgement involving men, 2 Peter has shown reluctance to dwell on their fate and has taken what opportunity there was to bring out the fact that God had mercy on any righteous man when he condemned the unrighteous of his generation. Thus he mentioned Noah as preserved in the time of the Flood, and Lot as preserved in the time when Sodom and Gomorrah were destroyed. If we are right in thinking that 2 Peter used Jude, this desire to dwell on the mercy of God as well as on his judgement may account for the omission of Cain and Korah, who were punished by God, and for reminding readers that Balaam was saved by 'the dumb beast' from doing the worst which he intended. It should be noticed that Balaam appears among the villains in both Letters. This is the character which he bears in Jewish tradition, as is explained below in the commentary on Jude 11 (p. 92).

We can now pass on to other apparent parallel passages in the two Letters:

Jude 9	2 Pet. 2: 11
In contrast, when the archangel Michael was in debate with the devil, disputing the possession of Moses's body, he did not presume to condemn him in insulting words, but said, 'May the Lord rebuke you!'	...whereas angels, for all their superior strength and might, employ no insults in seeking judgement against them before the Lord.

The most natural explanation of the likeness-with-difference here is that with his phrase 'for all their superior strength and might' 2 Peter has drawn out the meaning of Jude's reference to Michael, avoiding the lengthy argument with its quotation, which is not very neatly used by Jude.

Jude 10	2 Pet. 2: 12
But these men pour abuse upon things they do not understand; the things they do understand, by instinct like brute beasts, prove their undoing...	These men are like brute beasts, born in the course of nature to be caught and killed. They pour abuse upon things they do not understand; like the beasts they will perish...

2 Peter is most naturally understood as an expansion of Jude, introducing the further curious notion of 'like...beasts, born ...to be caught and killed'.

Jude 12	2 Pet. 2: 17a
clouds...without giving rain...	springs that give no water...

Jude 13	2 Peter 2: 17b
stars that have wandered from their course, and the place for ever reserved for them is blackest darkness...	the place reserved for them is blackest darkness...

Here it seems most natural to assume that 2 Peter has altered the rather unusual 'clouds...without rain' to the more familiar notion of 'springs that give no water' (everyone knew that some ran dry); this is more natural than to suppose that Jude altered a familiar and telling expression into an odd one. Again, if we compare Jude 13 with 2 Pet. 2: 17*b*, 'the place reserved for them is blackest darkness' is appropriate to 'stars that have wandered from their course' and would naturally be suggested by it (see the commentary on Jude 13). 'The place of blackest darkness' seems then to have been lifted by 2 Peter from Jude whom he has abbreviated, although in other places he adds a lot of material to his abbreviated version. This is exactly parallel to Matthew's treatment of Mark's gospel.

✳   ✳   ✳   ✳   ✳   ✳   ✳   ✳   ✳   ✳   ✳   ✳   ✳

A LETTER OF JUDE

'*Jude, servant of Jesus Christ*' (Jude 1)

✱ For the reasons which have been given in the previous pages it will be better to take the Letter of Jude first. It begins by claiming to be by 'Jude, servant of Jesus Christ and brother of James'. The natural way to take this would be to suppose that the author is Jude, the brother not only of James but also of Jesus himself (see the list of names in Mark 6: 3). In the New Testament there is indeed a Letter of James; in the commentary in this series on that Letter (*The Letters of John and James*) the difficult question of identifying the James of the letter is fully discussed (pp. 75–95, especially 93–5). The difficulty of holding that the Letter was written by James the brother of Jesus is explained. As is said there (p. 95), 'it would be a most extraordinary thing if while Jesus left no written works behind him, *two* of his brothers...had written considerable tracts, in the Greek language, and that these had been preserved, had come into general use about two hundred years after they were written, and been treated as canonical ever since'.

The Letter of Jude is mentioned first in the Muratorian Canon, which is a list of books of the New Testament compiled in about A.D. 190 (see *Understanding the New Testament*, p. 118). The earliest writers of the church to mention the Letter of Jude are Tertullian (*c.* 160–220), Clement of Alexandria (*c.* 150–215) and Origen (*c.* 185–254). Eusebius classifies books in the church as accepted, disputed (i.e. accepted by some but doubtful as to their origin) and rejected. He lists Jude as one of the disputed books, and remarks that few early writers refer to it (*Eccl. Hist.* 2. 23. 25 and 3. 25. 3). A number of considerations make it extremely unlikely that the Letter was written by the brother of Jesus himself; for example, in verse 4 the author condemns men 'whom Scripture long ago marked down for the doom they have incurred'. If he had been the brother of Jesus we should have expected him to say that Jesus had himself warned against the appearance of such men (he might have quoted Mark 13: 12 f. 'Brother will betray brother...', for example). More telling still, in verse 17 the author appeals to his 'friends', the readers, to 'remember the predictions made by the apostles of our Lord Jesus Christ'. Thus it is to them rather than to Jesus himself that he appeals as authority for his warnings. It is not surprising that nowhere does he claim to be the brother of Jesus, but claims to be the brother, as we have seen, of 'James', without saying who this James is.

The Letter is written to bring members of the church (not of a particular church only, but all 'those whom God has called') back to the 'defence of the faith, the faith which God entrusted to his people once for all'. This implies that the Christian church has been in existence long enough to become first settled in its teaching, and then to be influenced by some men whose teaching is not only wrong but evil and dangerous. 'Scripture...marked' them down 'long ago'. These hints, as well as the points made in the previous paragraph about the apostles as the authority for the church, all suggest a relatively late date for the Letter, about A.D. 100. It is usually regarded as the last book but one of the New Testament to be written, and 2 Peter as the last.

*   *   *   *   *   *   *   *   *   *   *   *   *

The Danger of False Belief

GREETING AND REASON FOR WRITING

1 FROM JUDE, servant of Jesus Christ and brother of James, to those whom God has called, who live in the love of God the Father and in the safe keeping of Jesus Christ.

2 Mercy, peace, and love be yours in fullest measure.

My friends, I was fully engaged in writing to you about 3
our salvation—which is yours no less than ours—when
it became urgently necessary to write at once and appeal
to you to join the struggle in defence of the faith, the
faith which God entrusted to his people once and for all.
It is in danger from certain persons who have wormed 4
their way in, the very men whom Scripture long ago
marked down for the doom they have incurred. They
are the enemies of religion; they pervert the free favour
of our God into licentiousness, disowning Jesus Christ,
our only Master and Lord.

* The author calls himself *Jude*, although we have seen
reason to doubt that he claims that he is the brother of Jesus
mentioned in Mark 6: 3. We need not doubt that his name
was Jude, and we can refer to him by this name, although
'Judas' is really more accurate and nearer the Jewish form of
the name. He seems to recall the Letter of James not only by
saying that he is his brother but also by calling himself simply
servant of Jesus Christ, and he does not add any claim to be an
apostle, because he lives in an age when they belong to the
past, as we have seen (see p. 82 and verse 17). The Letter of
James opens in a similar way with 'From James, a servant of
God and the Lord Jesus Christ'.

  1. In the phrase *those whom God has called* the word translated *called* is actually a noun and almost a technical term
meaning 'Christians'. Paul uses it (e.g. Rom. 1: 6, 'you who
have heard the call') but it is not used by the authors of the
Letters of Peter. The readers *live in the love of God*, that is,
their life as Christians is due to God's love which he has shown
in Christ; he does not mean the Christian's love for God.

  in the safe keeping of Jesus Christ: there is a hint here. The
readers will be safe if they remain in him and are not led
astray by the false teachers whom Jude is going to denounce.

It suggests also that they are being kept safe until Christ comes to take them into his kingdom. This is clear if we turn to verse 21, where the language used here is taken up again. The thought is an important part of the gospel in the early church, as for example when Paul says in Col. 3: 3 that 'your life lies hidden with Christ in God'.

2. The greeting is a Christian adaptation of the usual formal beginning of a letter of that time. An ordinary letter would begin with the name of the writer, then the name of the person to receive it, in a grammatical form which would be translated '*to* such-and-such a person'; this would be followed by a single word usually translated 'Greetings'. This last is so much a formality that it is missed out by the N.E.B. after the name 'Felix' in Acts 23: 26, although it is there in the Greek. In this letter of Jude we have already had the 'from' and 'to'; in this second verse we have a Christian equivalent of the formal 'Greetings': *Mercy, peace and love*, which is far from mere formality, for the words anticipate the content of the letter. The author wants God's mercy for his readers, though he fears judgement. Those who are leading them astray are causing division in the church, so *peace and love* are more than ever necessary. They are characteristics of the Christian life according to Paul in Gal. 5: 22 ('the harvest of the Spirit is love, joy, peace...').

3. *I was fully engaged in writing to you*: the N.E.B. has represented the Greek as though the writer was occupied with a larger treatise and broke off to write an urgent note which could be sent at once. If this is right, then the larger treatise might be 2 Peter, and the author who expanded Jude would then be the person who also wrote Jude. But it is uncertain if this is the true meaning, which may be rather 'being very eager to write to you...'.

It is interesting that Jude speaks of *our salvation* as though it were something almost tangible which can be guarded. In Paul it is something which God will give to the faithful at the end of the age. Here it is almost the same thing as the *faith*

mentioned at the end of the same verse; this word is used here
in the sense of a body of doctrine to be believed and preserved,
a meaning which is not far from some of the ways in which
Paul uses it, but for him, as for the church of his time, it
usually means trusting oneself to God in obedience; it is
includes belief that God has sent Jesus to be the Lord, but
not simply that belief. When people think about the *faith* as
Jude does here, the implication is that it can be defended by
argument, and this may be all that is necessary. But true
Christian faith can be 'defended' successfully only if it is lived
as well.

the faith which God entrusted to his people once and for all means
the right doctrine or system of belief. It is not the same as faith
as Paul understood and exemplified it, and as it is declared in
the great eleventh chapter of a Letter to Hebrews. Paul meant
more than that he had preserved the right doctrine, when he
wrote in 2 Tim. 4: 7 'I have kept faith', assuming this to be a
part of 2 Timothy actually written by Paul. Moreover, the
Christian church could not have lived but would have died
intellectually if it had been content to keep a body of doctrine
delivered to it *once and for all*. But Jude is right to call God's
people back to the right road. Thinking things out, and
seeing and expressing what our beliefs imply, is one thing;
but we ought not to accept teaching which is false and which
is morally harmful, and it is this teaching which Jude is
attacking.

4. *It is in danger from certain persons who have wormed their
way in*: Who were these? Clearly they were members of the
church although they do not deserve to be. It is possible that
they were travelling teachers such as Ignatius (*c.* 35–107)
knew to have attempted to seduce the Ephesian church of his
day from their loyalty (Ign. *Eph.* 7:1 and 9: 1). They seem
to have been people who had once been in the church and
then perhaps tried to take out of it with themselves a number
whom they had influenced by new teaching, like those who
'went out from our company, but never really belonged to

us; if they had, they would have stayed with us', as the author of 1 John 2: 19 puts it. But they may also have been false teachers still within the church, as we shall see.

The *Scripture* mentioned could be something written before the New Testament, for Jude was writing before the canon (list of accepted books) of the Old Testament was finally settled. See the note on Jude 14 (p. 95). In that case perhaps 1 Enoch is meant: this book was composed of different parts, of which chapters 37–71, usually known as the Book of Similitudes, may have been added as late as New Testament times. In that part, 1 Enoch 48: 10 says of the kings of the earth (who are regarded as enemies) that 'they have denied the Lord of Spirits and his anointed'—the sort of accusation brought at the end of the present verse of Jude, *disowning Jesus Christ*. In 1 Enoch 106: 19 and 108: 7*a* the belief is expressed that there are sinners whose names have been inscribed in a book in heaven, known to the angels. There are other passages in the Testaments of the Twelve Patriarchs, written some time around 130 B.C. or a little later, which are similar. For example, the patriarch Asher in the Testament of Asher 7: 5 is represented as warning his descendants, 'I have known that ye shall assuredly be disobedient, and assuredly act ungodly...' These writings must be considered seriously as the *Scripture* which is meant, because Jude actually quotes 1 Enoch 1: 9 in verse 14 below. The other possibility is made the more probable of the two by verses 17 f.; this is that the writings meant were books which we now have in the New Testament, writings of apostles or writings containing what apostles said. Thus there may well be a reference here to the words of Paul at Miletus according to Acts 20: 29 f.: 'I know that when I am gone, savage wolves will come in among you and will not spare the flock. Even from your own body there will be men coming forward who will distort the truth to induce the disciples to break away and follow them.'

they pervert the free favour of our God into licentiousness is not very clear. God's *free favour* is what is often called his *grace*, or free gift of forgiveness and of help to lead a better life after repentance. It is meant to spur the recipient to live in joyful obedience to God, but some people have taken advantage of the thought that God forgives them freely, and responded with the thought, 'Good! So we can do what we like!' Strange as it may seem, this was a real danger among some Christians, or rather among heretics from Christianity: they really believed that Christ had saved them from their sins, so now they engaged in a life of unbridled satisfaction of their appetites and lusts. Paul met this difficulty, as Rom. 6: 15 shows: 'Are we to sin, because we are not under law but under grace?'

If the N.E.B. footnote gives the right translation of the last words of the verse, 'disowning our one and only Master, and Jesus Christ our Lord', 'Master' means God and so two persons are meant. This will make the verse very like 1 Enoch 48: 10 quoted above, and suggests that, after all, 1 Enoch is the *Scripture* meant.

In the above section (verses 1–4) the verses are taken up in 2 Peter as follows: 2 by 2 Pet. 1: 2; 3 by 2 Pet. 1: 5; 4 by 2 Pet. 2: 1 ff. ✳

JUDGEMENTS BY GOD

You already know it all, but let me remind you how the 5 Lord, having once delivered the people of Israel out of Egypt, next time destroyed those who were guilty of unbelief. Remember too the angels, how some of them 6 were not content to keep the dominion given to them but abandoned their proper home; and God has reserved them for judgement on the great Day, bound beneath the darkness in everlasting chains. Remember Sodom and 7 Gomorrah and the neighbouring towns; like the angels, they committed fornication and followed unnatural lusts; and they paid the penalty in eternal fire, an example for all to see.

8 So too with these men today. Their dreams lead them to defile the body, to flout authority, and to insult
9 celestial beings. In contrast, when the archangel Michael was in debate with the devil, disputing the possession of Moses's body, he did not presume to condemn him in insulting words, but said, 'May the Lord rebuke you!'
10 But these men pour abuse upon things they do not understand; the things they do understand, by instinct
11 like brute beasts, prove their undoing. Alas for them! They have gone the way of Cain; they have plunged into Balaam's error for pay; they have rebelled like Korah, and they share his doom.

✻ 5. Who is *the Lord* here? If it means God, the meaning is quite straightforward. But the N.E.B. footnote tells us that some witnesses read 'Jesus'. It is not very likely that the author meant Joshua by this, even though, as the footnote says, it might be understood thus. The reference would then be to the destruction of Achan in Josh. 7. The reading 'Jesus' is hard to explain if it is not original, but a scribe might well alter it to 'the Lord' so as to mean God, recognizing that the author was referring to the Old Testament story. The explanation is an unexpected one: in 1 Cor. 10: 4 Paul shows that he thinks of Christ as being in the wilderness during the wanderings of the Israelites and playing a part in their story. He identified Christ with the rock from which they drank (see the commentary in this series on *1 and 2 Corinthians*, p. 73). Indeed, in a few (admittedly very few) witnesses God is not mentioned in 1 Cor. 10: 5 so that there too it would be Christ who punished the sinners in the wilderness. It seems quite probable that this is the meaning here and that we ought to read 'Jesus', not *the Lord*.

6. *the angels*: we are very familiar with the story that the entrance of sin and death into the world was due to the Fall of

Adam. That this myth is the most widely known in this connexion in all Christendom is due to Paul, who worked out its implications in Romans. But in New Testament times perhaps more emphasis was put on another myth as explanation of the evil in the world. This was the story told in Gen. 6: 1–4, and the most elaborate expansion of it available to us is in 1 Enoch 6 ff., whose account of the matter is very briefly summarized here in Jude. *Their proper home* was not only heaven but in the presence of God himself where the angels stood ready to receive his orders and go to carry them out. 1 Enoch 10: 4 gives the Lord's command to Raphael to 'bind Azazel hand and foot, and cast him into the darkness'. Azazel is one of the chief rebel angels, having taught mankind the arts of war and other skills which have led men into evil. According to Lev. 16: 8, 10, 26 he seems to have been thought of as a demon living in the wilderness.

7. *Sodom and Gomorrah and the neighbouring towns* may well have existed at the southern end of the Dead Sea, the story of their destruction in Gen. 19: 1–25 having a basis in fact—a volcanic disturbance. The names of the other towns were Admah and Zeboiim. The Dead Sea is 1,280 feet below sea level (i.e. the level of the oceans) and the deep valley in which it lies is very hot. Moreover, hot springs from the bottom of the sea make the water even hotter than it would be from the sun. The place caught the imagination of the author of 1 Enoch 67 where a vision granted to Noah is described: 'I saw that valley in which there was a great convulsion and a convulsion of the waters. And when all this took place, there was produced a smell of sulphur, and it was connected with those waters, and that valley of the angels who had led astray (mankind) burned beneath that land.' Like the author of this passage, Jude thinks of the punishment of the rebellious angels in connexion with that of the famous wicked cities, and perhaps thinks of the place as near those cities, just as 1 Enoch does.

Three judgements of God (the first perhaps thought of as carried out by Christ) have now been mentioned in these verses 5–7: Israel, angels, wicked cities. This number three is maintained in the argument which follows.

8. *these men today* are now shown to be guilty of exactly those sins which incurred the three judgements which have just been recalled. Israel is in verse 5 said to have been guilty of unbelief, but in 1 Cor. 10: 7 this is called idolatry, and it is expressed not only in false worship but in impure actions, for the 'play' in which they indulged according to Paul, who is quoting Exod. 32: 6, is fornication. So *these men...defile the body*. It was the special sin of the rebellious angels to *flout authority*. The men of Sodom and Gomorrah could be said to *insult celestial beings*, i.e. angels (in this case obedient ones) for two such stayed in the house of Lot, and the 'men of the city' demanded of Lot, 'Bring them out unto us that we may know them', where the word 'know' is a euphemism (Gen. 19: 1–5).

9. *In contrast*, Michael would not rebuke even the devil for, fallen and evil though the devil was, he was originally one of the celestial beings. The incident is described in a book which needs a little explanation: it was called The Assumption of Moses, but was apparently a composite work containing the Testament of Moses, which survives, and the Assumption (which means 'taking up', i.e. into heaven); this is almost wholly lost. It was in the part properly called Assumption of Moses that the incident recalled here is described, as we can tell from quotations from it in later writers. Moses has died and Michael is sent to take his body. The devil tries to refuse to allow this on the ground that he rules over the material world (of which the body of Moses would be a part), or on the ground that he could accuse Moses (the great function of the devil being to accuse men before God) of having struck the Egyptian (Exod. 2: 11 f.) and so being a murderer. As Moses was regarded as a holy being, the devil could be properly rebuked for this presumption and blasphemy, but Michael leaves it to the Lord to give the rebuke, since the devil is a celestial being, although of course a fallen one. *Michael* is the angel who is given the task of protecting Israel

and defending her when accused in the heavenly court. This is his role in Dan. 10: 13, 21; 12: 1 and in 1 Enoch, where he is always one of the highest angels. His position as the highest of all, as an archangel, is not found in every place where he is mentioned, but as the angel of Israel it is natural that he should often be thought of in this way. So he is *archangel* here and in 1 Thess. 4: 16. He seems to be the chief angel in Rev. 12: 7, where he and his angels wage actual war on the dragon, who stands there for the devil. See also the commentary on 1 Pet. 5: 8 (p. 70).

11. *the way of Cain* is the first of another group of three. Cain is well known to us as 'the first murderer' because of the famous story in Gen. 4: 1–15; but there is more to know about him in the tradition which lies behind this passage: in 1 John 3: 12 Cain is called 'a child of the evil one' and his nature, evil from the start, is the reason why he killed his brother. In the minds of those who in New Testament times interpreted the scriptures, this is no mere rhetoric; Cain was believed to have been conceived as the result of the devil's action which occasioned the expulsion of Adam and Eve from the Garden of Eden. There is in the Talmud even the belief that Cain was the result of a union of Eve with the serpent or devil. Cain was the first child born in the fallen state, and so was regarded as in some sense a 'child of the evil one' even if not literally so. The favour shown by the Lord to Abel showed that he on the other hand was righteous (Gen. 4: 4) and he is in some minds regarded as the prototype and the ancestor of all righteous men. Hence 'innocent Abel' may not be a full translation of the phrase in Matt. 23: 35; the words mean also 'righteous Abel'. The *way of Cain* is then indeed the way of murderers, but also of all wickedness and not only of murder. Philo, a Jew of Alexandria contemporary with the New Testament and much influenced by Greek philosophy, regards Cain as the leader and teacher of all who are in rebellion against God and sunk in their own self-absorbed sin.

The phrase *Balaam's error* may surprise us, because the story told in Num. 22–4 makes him blameless: he is hired by Balak to curse the Israelites but will not do so because God tells him to bless them instead. But the priestly editors of the Pentateuch (the first five books in the Bible) added something from a most interesting and unexpected tradition which had developed by their time. Num. 31 belongs to this stratum of tradition and verses 8 and 16 in that chapter are hostile to Balaam (for example, in Num. 31: 16 it is by Balaam's counsel that Israelites are tempted into idolatry; cf. also Josh. 13: 22). In the biblical narrative at Num. 24: 14 ff. Balaam advises Balak that Israel will destroy Moab in the future, but Jewish tradition represents him in several documents as having advised Balak how Israel's valour might be undermined by leading them into sin. This is only one of the examples of the way in which Balaam became in the Jewish imagination the very type of a wicked man whose wickedness took the form of hostility to Israel and of attempts to make them go wrong. Besides 2 Pet. 2: 15, Balaam is mentioned elsewhere in the New Testament only at Rev. 2: 14, where the author, in the spirit of Philo, regards Balaam as a good name for a false teacher, and recalls how the original Balaam 'taught Balak to put temptation in the way of the Israelites'. This is a reflexion not of the main biblical narrative, but, as we have seen above, of the Jewish tradition of the time when the New Testament was written. See the note on Rev. 2: 14 in the commentary on Revelation in this series, p. 27.

Korah is a straightforward case. In verse 8 men are condemned because they 'flout authority', and this authority was the authority of men in high positions in the church. In a parallel way Korah in Num. 16: 1–35 objected to the exclusive priestly authority of Moses and Aaron.

In the above section (verses 5–11) the verses are taken up in 2 Peter as follows: 5 by 2 Pet. 1: 12; 6 by 2 Pet. 2: 4 and 9; 7 by 2 Pet. 2: 6 and 10; 8 by 2 Pet. 2: 10; 9 by 2 Pet. 2: 11; 10 by 2 Pet. 2: 12. ✳

BEWARE OF FALSE TEACHERS

These men are a blot on your love-feasts, where they eat 12
and drink without reverence. They are shepherds who
take care only of themselves. They are clouds carried
away by the wind without giving rain, trees that in season
bear no fruit, dead twice over and pulled up by the roots.
They are fierce waves of the sea, foaming shameful deeds; 13
they are stars that have wandered from their course, and
the place for ever reserved for them is blackest darkness.

It was to them that Enoch, the seventh in descent from 14
Adam, directed his prophecy when he said: 'I saw the
Lord come with his myriads of angels, to bring all men 15
to judgement and to convict all the godless of all the
godless deeds they had committed, and of all the defiant
words which godless sinners had spoken against him.'

They are a set of grumblers and malcontents. They 16
follow their lusts. Big words come rolling from their
lips, and they court favour to gain their ends. But you, 17
my friends, should remember the predictions made by
the apostles of our Lord Jesus Christ. This was the 18
warning they gave you: 'In the final age there will be
men who pour scorn on religion, and follow their own
godless lusts.'

These men draw a line between spiritual and unspiritual 19
persons, although they are themselves wholly unspiritual.
But you, my friends, must fortify yourselves in your 20
most sacred faith. Continue to pray in the power of the
Holy Spirit. Keep yourselves in the love of God, and 21
look forward to the day when our Lord Jesus Christ in
his mercy will give eternal life.

22   There are some doubting souls who need your pity;
23   snatch them from the flames and save them. There are
others for whom your pity must be mixed with fear;
hate the very clothing that is contaminated with sensuality.
24   Now to the One who can keep you from falling and
set you in the presence of his glory, jubilant and above
25   reproach, to the only God our Saviour, be glory and
majesty, might and authority, through Jesus Christ our
Lord, before all time, now, and for evermore. Amen.

✵ 12. *These men are a blot* ('blots' would be better) *on your
love-feasts* because their presence, with its divisive influence,
spoils the harmony of the love-feast or eucharist which they
attend. This was the main meeting of the church, a meal
taken together during which the Last Supper and Jesus'
sacrificial death were recalled. Paul had occasion to rebuke the
Corinthians for their lack of harmony and fellowship in this
eucharistic gathering, at which the closest Christian unity
ought to be the most obvious feature. 'When you meet as a
congregation, it is impossible for you to eat the Lord's
Supper', he says (1 Cor. 11: 20) and after reminding them of
its origin he sternly declares, 'It follows that anyone who eats
the bread or drinks the cup of the Lord unworthily will be
guilty of desecrating the body and blood of the Lord'
(1 Cor. 11: 27).

They are shepherds who take care only of themselves, like those
of Ezek. 34: 2 in the chapter on which John 10: 14 ff. ('I am
the good shepherd...') is based. Those being rebuked may
then themselves be ministers in the church. The unfruitful
trees seem to recall those which fail 'to produce good fruit'
and are 'cut down and thrown on the fire' (Matt. 3: 10).

dead twice over is a strange expression. The idea of two
deaths is found in Rev. 2: 11; 20: 6, 15; 21: 8. There it is
quite intelligible: the first death is natural death, which may
be that of the martyr. This saves from the second death which

94

is the lot of the wicked and those who fall away in time of persecution; they are condemned to it at the final judgement which ends the period of a thousand years during which the martyrs reign, having been raised to life at the first resurrection. It is hard to imagine people *dead twice over* before they have died even once, and the explanation may be that they are so wicked that the writer sees them as destined for the second death already. This would be the more probable if he shared the belief found in 2 Pet. 2: 20, and perhaps most clearly in Heb. 6: 4-8 where it is said of those who were converted and experienced 'the spiritual energies of the age to come, and after all this have fallen away' that 'it is impossible to bring them again to repentance'. Such men were spiritually dead before they were converted and are now dead again, and Jude may mean just such men.

13. *stars that have wandered from their course* is used as a metaphor for those who have abandoned their true faith, for the planets were in the contemporary tradition identified with angels who had rebelled against the position in which they had been placed by divine authority; judgement in the form of destruction by fire is reserved for them (1 Enoch 18: 14 f.; 21: 3 ff.). This to us extraordinary notion proceeds from observing the heavens, which are taken to be intended to move in a perfectly orderly fashion expressing the design of God, the movements being controlled by angels allotted these tasks. The changeable movements of the planets were not understood, and so were attributed to the disobedience of these controlling angels. The author of the book 1 Enoch was one of those who believed that a solar calendar had been ordained by God, so that he disapproved of the phases of the moon nearly as much as of the wanderings of the planets. Jude sees the abyss of 1 Enoch in which the rebellious planet-angels are kept for their judgement as a place of *blackest darkness*.

14. In view of the foregoing comment and the frequent references to 1 Enoch, neither the mention of Enoch himself nor the quotation from 1 Enoch 1: 9 which we have here will

cause any surprise; but the treatment of the book as authoritative and as though it were on a level with any book of the Old Testament is an important fact and illustrates the state of the canon (the official list of books used by and read in the church) at this time. The canon included also a number of books written after those of our New Testament, and which afterwards fell out of favour, such as the Apocalypse (i.e. Revelation) of Peter and the Shepherd of Hermas (see *Understanding the New Testament*, pp. 105 ff.), as well as books written before New Testament times which continue the traditions of history, prophecy and wisdom of the Old Testament. Some of these were finally decided to be profitable for reading in church but not for the foundation of doctrine. They formed the Apocrypha, different branches of the church having different lists for this collection. Others remained outside any official collection. 1 Enoch seems to have been in the Greek Bible which was taken to Ethiopia with Christianity in the fifth century and for a long time 1 Enoch was known only in Ethiopic. The version of the Old Testament in that language lacked 1 to 4 Maccabees and Ezra-Nehemiah but contained Jubilees and 1 Enoch. The clear allusions to 1 Enoch in Jude 6 and 2 Pet. 2: 4, 9 f. and the quotation from it here in Jude 14 f. show that it was available in its Greek form during the first century A.D. and that it was highly regarded.

Enoch is *the seventh in descent from Adam* according to Gen. 5 ('the book of the generations of Adam'; see Gen. 5: 1 and 21). That 'God took him' (Gen. 5: 24) was taken as a mark of divine favour and of Enoch's status as a superior being.

16. *grumblers and malcontents*—not in an everyday sense, but like the Israelites in Exod. 15: 24 and 17: 3, for example, who grumbled against Moses, who had divine authority. *They follow their lusts* because they are rebellious against the ecclesiastical authorities, just as the Israelites in the wilderness rebelled against Moses and fell into uncleanness. *Big words*, i.e. proud and boastful words, typical of those who acknow-

ledge no authority over them. The phrase may be taken from the Assumption of Moses 7: 9.

17. *the predictions made by the apostles of our Lord Jesus Christ* are quoted as the final authority for not following the leadership of such men as are condemned here, and also as assurance to the faithful that such men's teaching and example does not mean the victory of evil: all this has been foreseen, and it is the duty of the faithful to stand fast.

the warning they gave you is given here as a quotation but it is not found in any known writing. It is a good summary of what must have been often spoken out loud in the churches and what is found in different words in Acts 20: 29 f. where Paul said to the members of the church at Miletus, 'when I am gone, savage wolves will come in among you.' See also I Tim. 4: I f., a very clear example from post-apostolic times, 'The Spirit says expressly that in after times some will desert from the faith and give their minds to subversive doctrines inspired by devils'. See also the commentary on I Pet. 2: 25.

19. The men against whom the readers are being warned are renegades; they had accepted the gospel but now have their own version of it. This is clearly implied in the quotation just given from I Tim. 4: I f. and is borne out by the description of them as men who *draw a line between spiritual and unspiritual persons*. It seems then that they were gnostics, inventors of strange systems of belief, into which adherents must be initiated in order to be enlightened enough to gain salvation. They divided men into the psychic (or natural) and the pneumatic (or spiritual). Paul makes a distinction which looks something like this in I Cor. 2: 14 f., but his contrast is between an 'unspiritual' man and one who has been given the Holy Spirit by God. The gnostics thought that they were 'spiritual' if they belonged to the few intellectually enlightened people who possessed their own special doctrines, which were often a strange mixture of philosophy and fantasy. Jude can see clearly the contrast between a man who thought of himself as 'spiritual' and boasted of it, and

one who relied on God's gift of the Holy Spirit; he can therefore pass from thinking of these so-called 'spiritual' people to urge his fellow-Christians *to pray in the power of the Holy Spirit*. The variant reading given in the N.E.B. footnote, 'these men create divisions; they are wholly unspiritual', may not be what Jude wrote but it conveys a point very neatly: these gnostic heretics 'create divisions' in the sense of dividing men into those whom they are pleased to regard as 'natural' and 'spiritual'; but the real divisions they make are in the church of God. They are therefore themselves *unspiritual* in the sense of Paul and Jude—they have not the gift of the Holy Spirit.

21. The gnostics here attacked sometimes taught that those who accepted their doctrines were thereby endowed with eternal life. Jude brings his readers back to the fundamental doctrine of the Christian Church, which is to *look forward to the day when our Lord Jesus Christ in his mercy will give eternal life*. In his time this *day* was still thought to be near, and disappointment that it was delayed was a great cause of the discontent and false teaching which Jude is correcting and which the author of 2 Peter attacks at greater length. Neither author provided an answer sufficient for modern times when the expectation of that *day* has to be considered afresh. This matter is discussed at length in the commentary on 1 Pet. 1: 3 ff. and in the essay, 'The Christian Hope', on p. 140.

It is interesting to see how the three 'persons' of the Trinity, as they later came to be called, are foreshadowed in the present passage, as in many other places in the New Testament. Here we have *the power of the Holy Spirit, the love of God* and *our Lord Jesus Christ in his mercy;* this may remind us of a number of passages, the most obvious being 2 Cor. 13 : 14, 'The grace of the Lord Jesus Christ, and the love of God, and fellowship in the Holy Spirit, be with you all', with which Paul closes his second letter to the Corinthians and which has been used as a prayer in the Christian church ever since.

22–3. Nothing of great importance is raised by the possible variant readings explained in the N.E.B. footnotes (*b*) 'There are some who raise disputes; these you should refute' and (c) 'some you should snatch from the flames and save'. By a combination of other readings than those adopted in the main text here, it would be possible to interpret Jude as meaning that even some of those who cause divisions may deserve to be saved out of pity. The general meaning seems to be that such a forgiving attitude is right towards any who have been for the time being misled by the false teachers, but who may be rescued. In approaching them, *hate the very clothing that is contaminated with sensuality* (i.e., be careful not to be drawn into their evil ways yourself). The leaders of these misguided ones are themselves due to be judged by God through his angels. It is part of the teaching of the Letter that their judgement must be left to these superior beings, and men must not presume to judge them. Thus while he has called them a 'blot on your love-feasts' our author does not say that they should be expelled from them (verse 12).

24–5. The final doxology is a very full and eloquent one, like Rom. 16: 25–7, which is probably later than Paul himself. Notice that the Christian is to expect to be *set . . . in the presence of his glory*. In Old Testament times a man appeared before God with a gift (i.e. a sacrifice), and the prophet Micah asks effectively, 'Wherewith shall I come before the Lord?', concluding that the gift must be that of an acceptable life (Mic. 6: 6–8). Several passages in the New Testament imagine the Christian at the end of the age appearing before God, and they exhort him to be ready for this. One example is Eph. 6: 10 ff. where great play is made with the word 'stand'. The Christian is to stand his ground 'and still to stand'; this translation of the last phrase is correct; but it probably means to 'stand before God', for it is envisaged that he will before this have 'completed every task'. In the above section (verses 12–25) the verses are taken up in 2 Peter as follows 12 by 2 Pet. 2: 13, 17; 13 by 2 Pet. 2: 17; 16 by 2 Pet. 2: 10, 18; 17 by 2 Pet. 3: 2; 24 by 2 Pet. 3: 14. ✻

✻   ✻   ✻   ✻   ✻   ✻   ✻   ✻   ✻   ✻   ✻   ✻   ✻

THE SECOND LETTER OF PETER

THE AUTHOR

The author calls himself Simeon Peter, a combination of names not found exactly in this form anywhere else. The use of Simeon, the correct Hebrew and Aramaic form by which Simon Peter would be called by his Jewish friends, as he is by James in Acts 15: 14, suggests a Jewish Christian setting. Since 2 Peter seems to have used Jude (see p. 77) and Jude itself belongs to that time after the apostles when they are regarded as the authorities of the past on whose work and prestige the church has been founded, 2 Peter cannot have been written by the apostle Peter himself. The Letter was regarded as doubtful in its authority in quite early times. Thus Origen (c. 185–254) is quoted by Eusebius (*Eccl. Hist.* 6.25.8) as having said in a part of his commentary on John, otherwise lost, 'Peter has left one epistle generally acknowledged, and it may be a second; for there is a doubt about it.' Eusebius himself says about 2 Peter that he has been led to regard it as uncanonical, and he drops a hint as to why it has survived: many thought it valuable and therefore gave it a place among 'the other scriptures'. He then goes on to reject quite confidently other writings attributed to Peter, such as the Gospel of Peter and the Revelation of Peter, and concludes his information about the writings of Peter by saying quite clearly, 'I recognize one epistle as genuine' (*Eccl. Hist.* 3. 3. 1–4). As we already know, elsewhere he includes among the disputed books the Letters of James and Jude, and 2 Peter (3. 25. 3).

The author of this Letter evidently faced the same problems as Jude, and seemed to wish to write a rather longer answer to those who were disturbing the church with both their doubts and their false teaching. Jude complains of 'danger from certain persons who have wormed their way in' (4), and 2 Peter (as we may conveniently call the author) of 'false teachers among you' who 'will import disastrous heresies'

(2: 1). Jude solemnly tells his readers that they 'should remember the predictions made by the apostles of our Lord Jesus Christ' (17) and 2 Peter echoes him with the words, 'Remember the predictions made by God's own prophets, and the commands given by the Lord and Saviour through your apostles' (3: 2). There are many other and very close parallels, most of which suggest an expansion of Jude by 2 Peter. They will be noticed as the book is read through, and are given in a table below. We conclude that the Letter was written about the end of the first century, even later than Jude, and that it is therefore the very last book to be written which was finally included in the canon of the New Testament.

PARALLELS BETWEEN JUDE AND 2 PETER

Jude	2 Peter
2 Mercy, peace, and love be yours in fullest measure	1:2 Grace and peace be yours in fullest measure
3 join the struggle in defence of the faith	1:5 try your hardest to supplement your faith
4 certain persons who have wormed their way in	2:1 you likewise will have false teachers among you
5 You already know it all, but let me remind you how the Lord...	1:12 ...I will not hesitate to remind you of this again and again, although you know it...
6 Remember too the angels, how some of them were not content to keep the dominion given to them but abandoned their proper	2:4 God did not spare the angels who sinned, but consigned them to the dark pits of hell, where they are re-served for judgement.

Jude	2 Peter
home; and God has reserved them for judgement on the great Day, bound beneath the darkness in everlasting chains.	2:9 Thus the Lord is well able to rescue the godly out of trials, and to reserve the wicked under punishment until the day of judgement.
7 Remember Sodom and Gomorrah and the neighbouring towns; like the angels, they committed fornication and followed unnatural lusts; and they paid the penalty in eternal fire, an example for all to see.	2:6 The cities of Sodom and Gomorrah God burned to ashes, and condemned them to total destruction, making them an object-lesson for godless men in future days.
8 So too with these men today. Their dreams lead them to defile the body, to flout authority, and to insult celestial beings.	2:10 Above all he will punish those who follow their abominable lusts. They flout authority; reckless and headstrong, they are not afraid to insult celestial beings....
9 In contrast, when the archangel Michael was in debate with the devil, disputing the possession of Moses's body, he did not presume to condemn him in insulting words, but said, 'May the Lord rebuke you!'	2:11 whereas angels, for all their superior strength and might, employ no insults in seeking judgement against them before the Lord.

Jude	2 Peter
10 But these men pour abuse upon things they do not understand; the things they do understand, by instinct like brute beasts, prove their undoing.	2:12 These men are like brute beasts, born in the course of nature to be caught and killed. They pour abuse upon things they do not understand.
12a These men are a blot on your love-feasts, where they eat and drink without reverence.	2:13 To carouse in broad daylight is their idea of pleasure; while they sit with you at table they are an ugly blot on your company, because they revel in their own deceptions.
12b–13 They are clouds carried away by the wind without giving rain, trees that in season bear no fruit, dead twice over and pulled up by the roots. They are fierce waves of the sea, foaming shameful deeds; they are stars that have wandered from their course, and the place for ever reserved for them is blackest darkness.	2:17 These men are springs that give no water, mists driven by a storm; the place reserved for them is blackest darkness.
16 …They follow their lusts. Big words come rolling from their lips,	2:18 They utter big, empty words, and make of sensual lusts

Jude	2 Peter
and they court favour to gain their ends.	and debauchery a bait to catch those who have barely begun to escape from their heathen environment.
17 But you, my friends, should remember the predictions made by the apostles of our Lord Jesus Christ.	3:2 Remember the predictions made by God's own prophets, and the commands given by the Lord and Saviour through your apostles.

The plan of the Letter is easily understood. The whole is best thought of as a *re*affirmation: some treacherous men have been leading others into the way of destruction and it is necessary to restate the Christian message. We can divide the Letter as follows:

   1: 1–19 Stand fast in true faith and practice.

1: 20 — 2: 22 Beware of those who are leading others astray.

   3: 1–18 Reaffirmation of the coming of the Day of the Lord.

✳ ✳ ✳ ✳ ✳ ✳ ✳ ✳ ✳ ✳ ✳ ✳

The Remedy for Doubt

STAND FAST IN TRUE FAITH AND PRACTICE

F ROM SIMEON PETER, servant and apostle of Jesus **1**
Christ, to those who through the justice of our God
and Saviour Jesus Christ share our faith and enjoy equal
privilege with ourselves.

Grace and peace be yours in fullest measure, through 2
the knowledge of God and Jesus our Lord.

His divine power has bestowed on us everything that 3
makes for life and true religion, enabling us to know the
One who called us by his own splendour and might.
Through this might and splendour he has given us his 4
promises, great beyond all price, and through them you
may escape the corruption with which lust has infected
the world, and come to share in the very being of
God.

With all this in view, you should try your hardest to 5
supplement your faith with virtue, virtue with knowledge,
knowledge with self-control, self-control with fortitude, 6
fortitude with piety, piety with brotherly kindness, and 7
brotherly kindness with love.

These are gifts which, if you possess and foster them, 8
will keep you from being either useless or barren in the
knowledge of our Lord Jesus Christ. The man who lacks 9
them is short-sighted and blind; he has forgotten how he
was cleansed from his former sins. All the more then, my 10
friends, exert yourselves to clinch God's choice and calling
of you. If you behave so, you will never come to grief.

11 Thus you will be afforded full and free admission into
the eternal kingdom of our Lord and Saviour Jesus
Christ.

* 1–2. Since the evidence seems to be overwhelming that
Simeon Peter, the name adopted by the author, is not really
his own name, what does he mean to convey by it? He has a
positive purpose, because he takes great care to speak as
though he were indeed Peter the apostle, as in 1: 14 ff. where,
for example, he says of the voice which according to the
gospels of Matthew, Mark and Luke was heard at the time
of the Transfiguration by Peter, James and John, 'This
voice from heaven we ourselves heard' (1: 18); again, in
3: 1 he says boldly, 'This is now my second letter to you...'
A clue lies in the Jewish cast of the name, Simeon Peter, and
in his addressing *those who...share our faith and enjoy equal
privilege with ourselves*. The real Peter, according to Acts
10: 1 — 11: 18, went through an experience which impressed
him very deeply and which convinced him with regard to the
Gentiles that 'God gave them no less a gift than he gave us
when we put our trust in the Lord Jesus Christ'. We may
guess then that the writer is addressing Gentiles in the name
of the Jewish Christians—or some of them. This interpretation is supported by the writer's including in his greeting
through the knowledge of God. This would have been unnecessary when writing to any who had been Jews before they
became Christians.

3–4. These verses have no parallel in Jude and are interesting
in that they show the influence of Hellenism. Where a
Christian, thinking in Jewish terms, would perhaps speak of
the Holy Spirit, 2 Peter writes *divine power*. Again, there is—
perhaps surprisingly—very little about *religion* in the Bible,
but 2 Peter commends *true religion*. Religion is man-made,
the gospel comes direct from God, and it is the gospel which
the New Testament proclaims and explains. Even *true
religion* (the word *true* is not in the Greek but the phrase well

represents the idea of the one Greek word) is a little strange
to the gospel. Similarly typical of Hellenism is the notion of
the corruption with which lust has infected the world. Both
Epicureanism and Stoicism (which Paul met in Athens,
Acts 17: 18) taught superiority over natural desires; Paul
evidently believed that 'the shackles of mortality' (Rom.
8: 21) were a result of the Fall of Adam, but Adam's sin was
not lust but disobedience, and the 'works of the flesh' (Gal. 5:
19, RSV) according to Paul are not connected with lust
but with a worldly outlook as opposed to a spiritual one. A
lofty remoteness from the natural desires of the body was an
injunction of Stoicism, whose aims included such detach-
ment from this world and its cares that the believer might
come to share in the very being of God; although the Stoics
thought of God differently from the Jews, it seems as if this
Jewish Christian Letter had been influenced by Stoicism here.

5–7. *faith* here is thought of in the same way as in Jude 3:
something to profess and argue about, this side of it being
emphasized more than the characteristic of faith which means
a self-entrustment to God. The word translated *supplement*
is the verb used of the action of citizens in ancient Athens who
provided the chorus in the drama festivals with their necessary
equipment; it came to mean 'supply' or 'provide' and is
found in a general sense elsewhere in the New Testament. It
is aptly used here: just as the chorus already existed but
needed supplementing with equipment, so *faith* is taken to
exist already but to need supplementing. The way in which
the readers are urged to *supplement* it is again very reminiscent
of Stoicism, which formed lists of desirable qualities, one of
which led to another, the chain of them forming a line of
advance. The chain here is full of Greek ideals, *virtue* being
in the hellenistic world right conduct under a discipline
accepted from a philosophy of life. It is by no means a typical
word in the Christian vocabulary, for the gospel lays the
emphasis on grace, the gift of God which alone enables the
recipient to please him.

Knowledge again is a typically Greek ideal: Plato believed that knowledge of the Good must affect the character of the seeker after knowledge, and his scheme of things as set out in his famous *Republic* tends to identify the good with the true. In this context this seems to afford the right interpretation, since it is unlikely that the author would intrude here any idea of *gnosis*, which was the pursuit of those very gnostic opponents whom he is writing to counteract. *Gnosis* for them meant knowledge in the sense of a secretly obtained and imparted special doctrine whose possession afforded salvation to the initiate. 2 Peter is thinking of that knowledge of the true and good which helps the possessor to lead a disciplined life. This is quite clear from the fact that in the chain this *knowledge* leads to *self-control*, another Stoic ideal, perhaps that most naturally associated with Stoics, and one which through their influence on Christianity has made many in the West almost identify Christianity with *self-control* in the sense of not showing emotions. The Stoics taught their adherents not to show emotion but were even more interested in *self-control* in its more natural sense—the control of one's life and instincts, living according to principle. *Fortitude* in times of adversity was a great ideal of the Stoics but the Greek word used here links the idea with the special Jewish and Christian virtue of endurance under persecution until the promised deliverance by God.

Piety here translates the Greek word rendered in verse 3 above by 'true religion', which gives its sense well: it means the attitude of reverence for God and respect for fellow-men which is sincere and so leads to *brotherly kindness*, the kindness felt towards those who are of the same family as oneself, the family in this case being all other disciples of Christ. *Love* comes at the end of the chain because it is the disposition which includes and surpasses all others. He who has *love* in the sense meant here is the complete Christian; for he acts always from a motive given by his devotion to God, and not from some disguised self-regarding motive. Hence its goodness is unconquerable; 'there is no limit to its faith, its hope, and its endurance' (1 Cor. 13: 7). It is therefore a true Christian insight which sees the chain beginning with *faith* and being completed by *love*. Paul says in Gal. 5: 6 that 'the only thing that counts is faith active in love' and Ignatius (*c.* 35–107), bishop of Antioch, wrote to the church at Ephesus when on his way to martyrdom at Rome, 'the beginning is faith and the end is love' (Letter to the Ephesians 14: 1).

8–9. These verses are most useful reminders to Christians: it is sometimes argued that according to Paul a Christian has only to trust in his redemption by Christ in order to be saved at the end of the age, and need not fear the results of his sins, if he commit any. Paul himself said enough to show how grossly this misrepresents his teaching; for example he roundly declares that 'we must all have our lives laid open before the tribunal of Christ, where each must receive what is due to him for his conduct in the body, good or bad' (2 Cor. 5: 10) and that God 'will pay every man for what he has done' (Rom. 2: 6). Some people seem to have misunderstood him, perhaps deliberately, as he himself suspects in Rom. 3: 8, where he complains that 'some libellously report' him 'as saying' '"do evil that good may come"', i.e. sin so that God may forgive by his grace. The author of the Letter of James had to meet such a misrepresentation of Paul, who would have agreed entirely with his insistence that 'faith divorced from deeds is lifeless as a corpse' (James 2: 26): 2 Peter enters here into the same controversy and teaches that the Christian must *foster gifts* such as he has just listed. One who fails to do this may think he can rely on his redemption because he has been baptized; but one who really thinks about his baptism will be led to cultivate and practise the Christian virtues. Baptism committed him to that, as 1 Peter taught and reminded his readers.

11. *the eternal kingdom of our Lord and Saviour Jesus Christ.* It is typical of the author that he should think of this kingdom

as equivalent to the kingdom of God, to live in which is the ultimate reward of the faithful. It is not the Messianic kingdom on earth, which is to come to an end 'when he (Christ) delivers up the kingdom to God the Father', as Paul says in 1 Cor. 15: 24. Thus he shows how little he distinguishes between Jesus and God. *

12 And so I will not hesitate to remind you of this again and again, although you know it and are well grounded in
13 the truth that has already reached you. Yet I think it right to keep refreshing your memory so long as I still lodge
14 in this body. I know that very soon I must leave it; indeed
15 our Lord Jesus Christ has told me so. But I will see to it that after I am gone you will have means of remembering these things at all times.

16   It was not on tales artfully spun that we relied when we told you of the power of our Lord Jesus Christ and his coming; we saw him with our own eyes in majesty,
17 when at the hands of God the Father he was invested with honour and glory, and there came to him from the sublime Presence a voice which said: 'This is my Son,
18 my Beloved, on whom my favour rests.' This voice from heaven we ourselves heard; when it came, we were with him on the sacred mountain.

19   All this only confirms for us the message of the prophets, to which you will do well to attend, because it is like a lamp shining in a murky place, until the day breaks and the morning star rises to illuminate your minds.

* 12. The writer's intention to remind his readers of what he knows they have already been taught is like Jude 5; both authors are trying to bring their readers back to the truth

they have been taught, and both adopt the device of bearing for this purpose the authority of a great name of the past. We have already seen that this method of writing was common at the time and we have mentioned the book called the Testaments of the Twelve Patriarchs in which each of the patriarchs gives a 'spiritual testament' to his descendants; that is, in view of his impending death he gives them spiritual instruction to keep and follow after he is gone. We saw (p. 12) that this was certainly a fashion of writing and that no one was meant to believe that the patriarchs had really written these 'testaments'. They are therefore called fictitious testaments; and it seems that we have the clearest evidence here that at any rate 2 Peter is such a 'fictitious testament': the early church did not everywhere believe that the letter was written by Peter, but here they read expressions which strongly implied it. They must therefore have accepted this device of writing, seeing it to be very like The Testaments of the Twelve Patriarchs in this important respect, that the author has a divine premonition that he is soon to die, and so gathers his sons to give them advice. So here the author, taking on the character of Peter, is determined to go on *refreshing* their *memory* so long as he is still in the *body*, and adds that he knows *that very soon* he *must leave it.*

14. *I know that very soon I must leave it; indeed our Lord Jesus Christ has told me so.* The alternative, 'I must leave it, as our Lord Jesus Christ told me', in N.E.B. footnote (*a*) points only to a difference of punctuation of the Greek and makes it even clearer that, in his assumed character as Peter, the author refers to what is implied in John 21: 18: '...when you are old you will stretch out your arms, and a stranger will bind you fast, and carry you where you have no wish to go'; in these words Jesus seems to prophesy Peter's martyrdom. As the next verse says, 'He said this to indicate the manner of death by which Peter was to glorify God' (John 21: 19). This was said in apparent contrast with what Jesus prophesied of the Beloved Disciple, which was 'If it should be my will that he

wait until I come, what is it to you?' (John 21: 22 and 23). As the Gospel according to John says, this caused a rumour that the Beloved Disciple was destined not to die. According to this passage of the gospel Peter was to die in his old age. 2 Peter therefore writes in the character of the apostle near the end of his life. It is interesting that he refers to the tradition in John 21. It is quite probable that he knew it as a sacred writing; this would be another indication of the lateness of 2 Peter.

15. *after I am gone you will have means...* suggests that the author sees his present work as something to take his place *after I am gone*. This makes the best sense in the simplest way; it is unnecessary to suppose that any other work is meant, such as the gospel of Mark, since the author did not necessarily know of the traditional connexion of Peter with it (see p. 11); nor is it necessary to refer to any of the later writings such as the Gospel of Peter or the Apocalypse of Peter, for we do not know whether the author had any acquaintance with these or with anyone who intended to write them.

16–18. 2 Peter, speaking boldly in his character as the real Peter, despises *tales artfully spun* as did contemporary historians who like him claimed to give the real facts; but he has in mind especially the 'myths' *spun* by gnostic teachers such as are mentioned in 1 Tim. 1: 4 and 4: 7 (the Greek word for tales here is the same as 'myths'). Although he may not be the real Peter, he does stick to the facts of the gospel, as he claims, and as many writers in the New Testament insist that they do. Thus Luke claims to give 'authentic knowledge' (Luke 1: 4) and 1 John opens with a remarkable passage containing such words as 'What we have seen and heard we declare to you' (1 John 1: 3). Nevertheless it is chiefly of the risen Lord that the author here speaks: *the power of...Christ* is that which has been given him by his resurrection. Paul calls Jesus 'the power of God' in 1 Cor. 1: 24 and 2: 5, meaning that in Jesus and his crucifixion power has been gained over the evil forces of this world. In that passage the resurrection is not mentioned but everywhere supposed. Moreover, again and again we meet the conviction that God has given *power* to the risen Lord and set him on a throne over his enemies. Matt. 28: 18 sums this up by making the risen Lord say, 'Full authority in heaven and on earth has been committed to me.'

his coming is no less important: we have seen that all the writings in the New Testament came into existence through men who believed that the age was soon to come to an end and that Jesus would return in power to vindicate his own and to judge the world (p. 19). The writer claims *we saw him with our own eyes* because Peter, James and John were the only witnesses of the Transfiguration as it is told in the synoptic gospels (Mark 9: 2–8; Matt. 17: 1–8; Luke 9: 28–36). *Majesty* means that Jesus was seen in his divine nature. Mark 9: 2 says, 'In their presence he was transfigured', and the word 'trans-figured' means that his form was changed. Phil. 2: 6 says 'the divine nature was his from the first', translating a Greek phrase which literally means 'being in the form of God'. However we understand these mysteries, it is clear that New Testament writers believed that Jesus had a divine form or nature, which could be and was made visible. 2 Peter inter-prets the making visible of Jesus' divine nature a little differ-ently by saying that on this occasion of the Transfiguration Jesus *was invested with honour and glory* by *God the Father*. He is able to say this because in the gospel story a cloud is present from which the divine voice comes. This cloud is that which often accompanied the divine presence in the Old Testament. To take but one example, Exod. 24: 16 says, 'And the glory of the Lord abode upon mount Sinai, and the cloud covered it six days; and the seventh day he called unto Moses out of the midst of the cloud.' This glory and cloud are to the Jewish scholars who interpreted the scriptures much the same: they signify the *Presence* (Hebrew, *shekinah*) of God. The Greek word which corresponds is that for *glory*, translated thus in the first part of the verse, but certainly meaning *Presence* where it is so rendered. The words of the divine *voice* are the same as in

Matt. 17: 5 in the text adopted by the N.E.B., but Mark, Matthew and Luke all add 'listen to him'. They are not important to 2 Peter's argument here because he is emphasizing the reality of the risen Lord and his imminent coming, not his teaching.

17. The N.E.B. gives in the footnote an alternative translation 'This is my only Son' for *This is my Son, my Beloved.* This is not due to an alternative reading but is another way of rendering the same words, because the word usually translated 'beloved' sometimes carries with it the sense of 'the only one'—therefore all the more precious. Doubt how to translate the word when applied to Jesus as God's son reflects the thought that God has called us all to be his sons and daughters, yet Jesus is his only true son. The Gospel according to John gets over this by using a word translated in older versions (A.V. and R.V., for example) 'only begotten' (e.g. John 1: 18). Jesus is God's son by nature, others by union with Jesus. Paul says in Gal. 4: 4 f., 'God sent his own Son...in order that we might attain the status of sons.'

18. 2 Peter repeats his claim that this is no 'tale' with the words *we ourselves heard.* It is interesting that what in the gospels was just a mountain, though a very high one, has become in the course of time *the sacred mountain.* There is no indication in the New Testament as to which mountain it was; Mount Tabor is nowadays pointed out to travellers as the mount of the Transfiguration, but this is very unlikely since there were settlements on its summit in New Testament times.

19. If the vision and message from the voice of God at the Transfiguration *confirms for us the message of the prophets* we have here a simple statement proceeding from the belief which we have already met, that the whole New Testament story had been somewhere prophesied in the scriptures, i.e. the Old Testament (p. 20). Curiously enough, the Greek almost certainly means what is given in the N.E.B. footnote, 'And in the message of the prophets we have something still more certain', implying that the prophets' testimony to Jesus was

'more certain' than the voice of God at the Transfiguration. There is, however, no real problem: the writer means that the prophets are an even stronger witness to the fact that the exalted Lord Jesus is destined to come in power at the end of the age; the Transfiguration showed that only by implication, by revealing what Jesus was destined to be like in eternity. The claim to have seen him 'in majesty' (verse 16) is a claim to have seen him as he will be at 'his coming'. It is this, not a general testimony to the divine nature of Jesus, which receives even stronger, because more direct, support from the prophets.

In almost all instances of the use of the word meaning *morning star* in antiquity, the planet Venus is meant. Jesus at his coming is compared to this herald of the new day. Another and perhaps more likely explanation is that Num. 24: 17, 'There shall come forth a star out of Jacob', was considered in both Judaism and Christianity as a text about the Messiah; it is therefore natural that Jesus should be called a star here and in Rev. 22: 16 ('the bright morning star'). Nevertheless, he is called this when his future coming is much in mind. It is very striking that the author should think not only of Jesus coming like a star to vindicate his people and to judge, but thinks of this great day as that on which *the morning star rises to illuminate your minds*. The words and the idea remind us of Luke 1: 78 f.:

'...in the tender compassion of our God
        the morning sun from heaven will rise upon us,
to shine on those who live in darkness, under the cloud of
        death,
        and to guide our feet into the way of peace.'

The passage therefore shows considerable reflexion upon the last day and does not think of it only in a crude way as the end of the age. Rather is it the day when a great transformation will take place in the *minds* of men. ✻

1 : 20—2 : 22   BEWARE OF THOSE WHO ARE
LEADING OTHERS ASTRAY

FALSE TEACHERS

20 But first note this: no one can interpret any prophecy of
21 Scripture by himself. For it was not through any human
whim that men prophesied of old; men they were, but,
impelled by the Holy Spirit, they spoke the words of
God.

2   But Israel had false prophets as well as true; and you
likewise will have false teachers among you. They will
import disastrous heresies, disowning the very Master
who bought them, and bringing swift disaster on their
2 own heads. They will gain many adherents to their
dissolute practices, through whom the true way will be
3 brought into disrepute. In their greed for money they
will trade on your credulity with sheer fabrications.

But the judgement long decreed for them has not been
4 idle; perdition waits for them with unsleeping eyes. God
did not spare the angels who sinned, but consigned them
to the dark pits of hell, where they are reserved for
5 judgement. He did not spare the world of old (except for
Noah, preacher of righteousness, whom he preserved
with seven others), but brought the deluge upon that
6 world of godless men. The cities of Sodom and Gomorrah
God burned to ashes, and condemned them to total
destruction, making them an object-lesson for godless
7 men in future days. But he rescued Lot, who was a good
man, shocked by the dissolute habits of the lawless society
8 in which he lived; day after day every sight, every sound
9 of their evil courses tortured that good man's heart. Thus

the Lord is well able to rescue the godly out of trials, and
to reserve the wicked under punishment until the day of
judgement.

✶ 1: 20–1. *no one can interpret any prophecy of Scripture by
himself* is a warning not so much that the individual must
accept the authority of the church as that he must remember
that he needs the *Holy Spirit*, just as the prophecies themselves
owe their origin not to mere *human whim* but to the Holy
Spirit. The notion that a special gift was needed to unlock the
real meaning hidden in the prophets was shared by the men of
Qumran (a monastic sect of strict Jews who lived by the
Dead Sea and whose scrolls were discovered in 1947 and
following years), who applied prophecies to their own history
and obtained thereby a conviction about what was due to
happen in the immediate future. The early church made the
same mistake about some prophecies, taking them too
literally, or else in a fanciful way, but was right in seeing that
Christ was the clue to the Old Testament hopes and
expectations.

2: 1. The Holy Spirit is needed both to utter and to
interpret the prophecies, but both those who utter them and
those who interpret may be mistaken or may deliberately
deceive others about possessing the Holy Spirit. The *false
prophets* of old Israel are balanced by *false teachers* at the time
2 Peter is being written. The 'persons who have wormed their
way in', as Jude 4 expresses it, *will import disastrous heresies.*
The language here is very similar and we are reminded that
these probably gnostic teachers are guilty of *disowning the very
Master who bought them.* See the footnote on Jude 4, in which
passage there is no reference to the redemption wrought by
the *Master* as there is here. The words *who bought them* are a
very correct translation and the Greek is a bold metaphor
standing for the usual 'redeemed', which does literally mean
'bought back' but is more often used as a metaphor in the
New Testament than the plain word 'bought'.

2. *They will gain many adherents to their dissolute practices:*
these are those false teachers who persuaded people that,
being now redeemed by Christ and living in the spirit, they
could disregard moral scruples and live as they wished as far
as their everyday lives were concerned. Such teaching led to
moral laxity and was one of the extreme results of gnosticism.
The other extreme possibility was asceticism of such an acute
kind that marriage was forbidden, and the life of the flesh
regarded as evil in itself. Both kinds had to be resisted, as we
know from Paul's careful arguments in 1 Cor. 7 and from
1 Tim. 4: 1 ff.

the true way will be brought into disrepute because to the out-
sider all will be thought of as Christians, especially as those
who taught and practised such a perversion of Christianity
claimed to be part of the church; they 'wormed their way
in' and 'imported disastrous heresies'.

3. *In their greed for money*: the type of teacher now being
condemned seems to have established a position in the
churches after the apostles were dead and leadership fell upon
the shoulders of local members. Thus the Pastoral Letters
(1 Timothy, 2 Timothy and Titus) are written to re-establish
the honour of the ministry and at the same time to insist that
only men of good character be chosen for the different orders.
Since it was a principle of the church that its teachers should
be supported by its members, it was possible for some to seek
office for the money. Titus 1: 10 f. describes such men who
'talk wildly and lead men's minds astray'. Like those attacked
here in 2 Peter and in Jude, they do it 'by teaching things they
should not, and all for sordid gain'. Such men could *trade on*
others' *credulity* the more easily if they persuaded them to
live lives of low pleasures.

4. As is fully explained in the commentary on 1 Pet.
3: 19 (p. 51), there is there, in Jude 6 and here in 2 Peter a
reference to 1 Enoch 10: 11–14, where disobedient spirits
('fallen angels') are consigned to the abyss to await judgement.

5. *the world of old* presented 'types', i.e. events understood

to foreshadow those to come; the final judgement is thought to be prefigured by the judgement at the Flood, which is a 'type' of the final judgement itself (see p. 53). We find this idea also in Luke 17: 26 f. and Matt. 24: 37 ff. ('As things were in Noah's days, so will they be when the Son of Man comes'). Although 2 Peter seems to follow Jude here, he inserts a reference to Noah, the first of his exceptions to the judgements which destroyed the wicked. Noah's character as a *preacher of righteousness* is found not in the Old Testament but in such books as Jubilees; in Gen. 7: 1 the Lord does indeed say to Noah 'thee have I seen righteous before me in this generation' but later ages built up his character as a lawgiver to his people. 1 Enoch contains fragments of a lost Book of Noah written in the early part of the intertestamental period and in one of the Qumran scrolls, A Genesis Apocryphon, he is so far the hero that his birth is under divine providence and he is a remarkable infant as soon as he is born. (The Genesis Apocryphon can be found, with explanations, in Vermès, *The Dead Sea Scrolls in English*, Pelican, 1962.)

seven others: these were Noah's wife, his three sons, Shem, Ham and Japheth, and their wives (Gen. 7: 7, 13). With Noah himself they make the eight specially mentioned in 1 Pet. 3: 20.

6. *Sodom and Gomorrah* are mentioned in a similar way in Jude 7, but here their character as a 'type' of the final judgement is even clearer. We may compare Jubilees 16: 6, 9; there Sodom is made to seem incapable of being redeemed, for Abraham's intercession for the city (Gen. 18: 20–33) is omitted by the author, who is writing a modified version of the Genesis stories. Thus Sodom and Gomorrah and their fate become pure 'types' or in this case *an object-lesson for godless men in future days*.

7–9. Gen. 19 does not specially give the impression that Lot *was a good man*. The picture of him here as one greatly troubled by the wickedness around him is found also in Wisd. 10: 6 (written a little before New Testament times), where the Greek, as here, describes him as 'righteous' and says that Wisdom rescued him 'while the ungodly were perishing'. 2 Peter uses some imagination to make the point summed up in 1 Clement 11: 1 (about A.D. 93): 'Lot for his hospitality and piety was saved from Sodom, when all the neighbourhood was judged by fire and brimstone. The Lord made plain thereby that he deserts not those that hope in him, but those who are renegades he gives over to punishment and torture.' In the same way, in verse 9, 2 Peter says the Lord is well able to rescue the godly out of trials, and to reserve the wicked under punishment until *the day of judgement*. The assurance to the righteous that they will be rescued is an addition to the message given at this point by Jude. In Rom. 8: 31–9 we find Paul devoting much eloquence to reassuring his readers in their apparent fear of the final judgement. 'If God is on our side, who is against us?' he asks. It should be noticed that 2 Peter believes, along with the Jews of his day, that the wicked are not only reserved for punishment but until the day when they are condemned to it they are *under punishment*, like the rich man in Jesus's story in Luke 16: 19–31. This is entirely consistent with the theme that God anticipates his final judgement in special acts in history: the wicked who do not appear to suffer any judgement from God during their lifetime are thought to meet it when they die. ✻

MEN OF LUST

10 Above all he will punish those who follow their abominable lusts. They flout authority; reckless and headstrong,

11 they are not afraid to insult celestial beings, whereas angels, for all their superior strength and might, employ no insults in seeking judgement against them before the Lord.

12   These men are like brute beasts, born in the course of nature to be caught and killed. They pour abuse upon

things they do not understand; like the beasts they will perish, suffering hurt for the hurt they have inflicted. To 13 carouse in broad daylight is their idea of pleasure; while they sit with you at table they are an ugly blot on your company, because they revel in their own deceptions.

They have eyes for nothing but women, eyes never at 14 rest from sin. They lure the unstable to their ruin; past masters in mercenary greed, God's curse is on them! They have abandoned the straight road and lost their way. 15 They have followed in the steps of Balaam son of Beor, who consented to take pay for doing wrong, but was 16 sharply rebuked for his offence when the dumb beast spoke with a human voice and put a stop to the prophet's madness.

These men are springs that give no water, mists driven 17 by a storm; the place reserved for them is blackest darkness. They utter big, empty words, and make of sensual 18 lusts and debauchery a bait to catch those who have barely begun to escape from their heathen environment. They promise them freedom, but are themselves slaves 19 of corruption; for a man is the slave of whatever has mastered him. They had once escaped the world's 20 defilements through the knowledge of our Lord and Saviour Jesus Christ; yet if they have entangled themselves in these all over again, and are mastered by them, their plight in the end is worse than before. How much 21 better never to have known the right way, than, having known it, to turn back and abandon the sacred commandments delivered to them! For them the proverb 22 has proved true: 'The dog returns to its own vomit', and, 'The sow after a wash rolls in the mud again.'

✻ 10–11. The story of Sodom and Gomorrah makes it easy for the author to insist that *Above all he will punish those who follow their abominable lusts*. It is perhaps worth while to remind ourselves that the author does not, any more than any other teacher in the New Testament, condemn the natural life of the 'flesh'. The Jewish way, inherited by the early church, held marriage in honour. Tobias in the book of Tobit approaches his bride on his wedding night with a prayer, 'O Lord, I take not this my sister for lust, but in truth' (Tobit 8: 7). It is the unregulated and undisciplined life of the body (whether it be the appetite of hunger, thirst, or any other natural appetite like sex which is being considered) which is condemned. *They flout authority* naturally enough, because they have thrown over all discipline. That they do this and that they *insult celestial beings* is the accusation of Jude 8, where the note explains what is meant. In Jude 9 Michael is the angel who provides an example of one who is careful to *employ no insults in seeking judgement against them*, and the matter is explained in the note on that passage (see p. 90 f.).

12–13. The comparison with *brute beasts* is found also in Jude 10, but elaborated here by the thought that they are destined *to be caught and killed*. Jude 12 said of such men that they were a 'blot on your love-feasts' and this was taken to mean that they were unworthy partakers of the love-feasts of the church which contained the origin of the Eucharist. According to the reading adopted by the N.E.B., 2 Peter alters this slightly to saying that such men are a *blot on your company*, that is on the church itself, thus confirming the impression gained from Jude that such men were members of the church whose expulsion was not demanded but whose influence must be resisted. It may be that 2 Peter originally said the same, for the word for *deceptions* in the oldest Greek manuscripts would look very like the word for love-feasts. The N.E.B. footnote shows that some manuscripts actually give the word which would make the passage mean 'in their love-feasts', making the passage even nearer to Jude 12.

The other alternative, mentioned also in the footnote, is to suppose that the author wrote *deceptions* but was thinking particularly of *love-feasts* and of the likeness between the two Greek words. The only way to render this in English is by some such phrase as is suggested in the footnote, 'in their mock love-feasts', or by a corresponding pun in English, which is hard to invent.

14. The translation is rather free, a necessary method of rendering slightly involved Greek which, literally taken, says that these men's eyes are 'full of an adulteress and unceasing from sin', reminding us of Jesus's teaching, 'If a man looks on a woman with a lustful eye, he has already committed adultery with her in his heart' (Matt. 5: 28).

15. *the straight road* (same word as *way* in Greek) is the way of Christianity, which is called this in Acts, e.g. 9: 2 and 24: 14. In John 14: 6 it is claimed that Jesus is himself the way, because Christianity is summed up in him—in his teaching and in following the path he pioneered.

The reason why Balaam is regarded as such a villain is explained in the note on Jude 11, where he appears in the same character. There Cain and Korah were held up with him as bad examples. 2 Peter takes only Balaam and develops this theme. That he *consented to take pay* may seem strange in view of Num. 22: 17 f. where Balaam most honourably refuses to take a bribe from Balak to curse Israel, but these very verses were turned against him in commentaries by the rabbis. In the story in Numbers he says, 'If Balak would give me his house full of silver and gold, I cannot go beyond the word of the Lord my God...' and, by taking the first part of the verse by itself, this is taken to mean that Balaam coveted silver and gold. It is necessary to remember that Balaam was an arch-villain in contemporary Jewish imagination to see why those who have *followed in* his *steps* are tantamount to the ungodly. This point of view is well illustrated by a passage in a collection of sayings of rabbis of various dates, some of them contemporary with the New Testament and collected together by about A.D. 200. This collection is called *Pirqè 'Aboth* or Sayings of the Fathers. In 5: 22 of this book we read a passage which has many parallels with Jude 11–13, but especially with 2 Pet. 2: 10–22: 'Every one who has three things is one of the disciples of Abraham our father. And every one who has three other things is one of the disciples of Balaam the wicked. If he has a good eye, and a lowly soul and a humble spirit, he is of the disciples of Abraham our father. If he has an evil eye, and a boastful soul and a haughty spirit, he is of the disciples of Balaam the wicked. What is the difference between the disciples of Abraham our father and the disciples of Balaam the wicked? The disciples of Balaam the wicked inherit Gehenna and go down to the pit of destruction...' The evil eye is the theme of verse 14, and that such men are boastful and haughty is shown in 2 Peter by the fact that 'they utter, big empty words' (verse 18).

16. 2 Peter adds to Balaam's disgrace by showing that he *was sharply rebuked* by a *dumb beast*. This was the donkey on which Balaam rode and which saw the angel of the Lord blocking the way, although Balaam could not see the angel himself until the Lord opened his eyes for the purpose, thus vindicating the donkey which had by now protested at Balaam's blows (Num. 22: 22 ff.). The Lord had 'opened the mouth of the ass', i.e. given her for the moment *a human voice*. Indeed, in the story the donkey argues in a rational way, in marked contrast to *the prophet's madness*.

17. *springs that give no water* and *mists driven by a storm* are meant to give the same sort of impression as 'the clouds carried away by the wind without giving rain' in Jude 12, metaphors very telling in a dry climate. Another parallel with the passage from *Pirqè 'Aboth* is seen in the fate *reserved for* the disciples of Balaam, *blackest darkness* which is the same as the 'pit of destruction'. Cf. Jude 13.

18. That these men, within the Christian church but a 'blot' on it, could *make lusts and debauchery* a bait is surprising. It is due to the perversion of the gospel discussed in the note

on 1: 8–9 which could be summed up in the words, 'Christ has saved me from my sins—so now I can do what I like!' That those caught were those who had *barely begun to escape from their heathen environment* is very easy to understand. When they became Christians they were offered salvation from their past sins. This was welcome; not so welcome was the duty to 'supplement...faith with virtue' (1: 5) for those who were not really in earnest, because this meant self-discipline. To be told they were now free to do what they liked would be more welcome than anything else if their hearts and minds in themselves were not truly changed.

19. Thus the wicked men *promise them freedom;* but to give oneself over to a life of lust is to be a slave to it like being a slave to a drug. Their false leaders are themselves in this state and so are *slaves of corruption.* This is very seriously meant. 2 Peter evidently believed, as we saw in 1: 4, that lust had 'infected the world' with 'corruption', as though moral failure, especially in the sphere of sexual life, was the cause of corruption in the physical sense of decay or liability to decay. That *a man is the slave of whatever has mastered him*, especially if it be sin which has mastered him, is taught firmly by Paul, who says in Rom. 6: 20, for example, 'When you were slaves of sin, you were free from the control of righteousness; and what was the gain? Nothing but what now makes you ashamed, for the end of that is death.' It is taught also in John 8: 34 where Jesus says, 'everyone who commits sin is a slave.'

20. *They had once escaped* by leaving their former life and being baptized. *The knowledge of our Lord and Saviour Jesus Christ* is of the kind which can be possessed only by one who believes in Christ. The word for *knowledge* here includes the sense of acknowledgement, and is the same word as is used in 1 Tim. 2: 4. There it is God himself who is called Saviour, 'whose will it is that all men should find salvation and come to know the truth', the Greek there meaning, literally, 'come to knowledge of the truth'. Such knowledge is not only

intellectual but helps to describe the condition of its holder. *Their plight in the end is worse than before* not only because of the strong tendency to believe that there could be no repentance after baptism (as Heb. 6: 4 ff. argues, when men have received so much from God 'and after all this have fallen away, it is impossible to bring them again to repentance'); the argument assumes that deliberate rejection of so much good, and that a divine gift, must mean the possession of a heart incapable of the necessary repentance. It is the sin of falling away (the technical term is 'apostasy') which is being discussed, not the many thoughtless sins which all Christians commit, but for which they can properly express repentance and be forgiven again. The words here in 2 Peter also recall Matt. 12: 45: 'in the end the man's plight is worse than before.' The man described there is one who has been liberated from one evil spirit and remained empty until seven others worse than the first enter him. Although in Jesus' saying the remaining empty is not perhaps made the central point of a rather strange story, it is natural to think that the man might have been defended by the presence of the Spirit of God within him, and the armour which God would supply. 2 Peter seems to teach such a lesson with his insistence on the importance of cultivating virtues (1: 5 ff). It is striking that the apostate (the Christian who has fallen away) is not back where he started but *worse than before;* it is a greater sin to reject the good when you have known it than to live in wickedness when you did not know the power for good available from God.

21. This is why it is *much better never to have known the right way, than...to turn back. The right way* has here a very definite meaning: it is the whole Christian life, the same thing as 'righteousness' in 1 Pet. 2: 24 and 'your virtues' (the Greek is 'righteousness') in 1 Pet. 3: 14. The N.E.B. at Matt. 5: 20 gives the rendering 'unless you show yourselves far better men than the Pharisees', the Greek being literally 'unless your righteousness excel...', showing that righteous-

ness means the whole way of life, as it does here, and so is rightly translated *the right way*.

Jude 3 speaks of 'the faith which God entrusted to his people once and for all'. The language here in 2 Peter is very similar, but he speaks not of the 'faith' but of *the sacred commandments delivered to* Christians. These are not the Ten Commandments but 'the commands' mentioned in 3: 2 below, where they are explained.

22. *The dog* and *the sow* are both unclean animals to Jews; when they used the word 'dogs' they sometimes meant Gentiles, signifying that they were unclean and not to be associated with. Here it is moral uncleanness which is meant, and the proverb about *the dog* is to be found in Prov. 26: 11. There are a number of similar sayings about *the sow* in pagan authors but this particular one has not been found elsewhere. ✶

REAFFIRMATION OF THE COMING OF
THE DAY OF THE LORD

SOME DIFFICULTIES ANSWERED

This is now my second letter to you, my friends. In both of **3** them I have been recalling to you what you already know, to rouse you to honest thought. Remember the predic- 2 tions made by God's own prophets, and the commands given by the Lord and Saviour through your apostles.

Note this first: in the last days there will come men who 3 scoff at religion and live self-indulgent lives, and they 4 will say: 'Where now is the promise of his coming? Our fathers have been laid to their rest, but still everything continues exactly as it has always been since the world began.'

In taking this view they lose sight of the fact that there 5 were heavens and earth long ago, created by God's

6 word out of water and with water; and by water that
7 first world was destroyed, the water of the deluge. And
the present heavens and earth, again by God's word, have
been kept in store for burning; they are being reserved
until the day of judgement when the godless will be
destroyed.

8   And here is one point, my friends, which you must not
lose sight of: with the Lord one day is like a thousand
9 years and a thousand years like one day. It is not that the
Lord is slow in fulfilling his promise, as some suppose,
but that he is very patient with you, because it is not his
will for any to be lost, but for all to come to repentance.

* When the author says *This is now my second letter to you,
my friends*, this is no proof that he really was Peter (see p. 106)
for we know that such evidence was not accepted by many
in the early church (see p. 100). In the commentary on 1: 12 it
was explained that at that point the character of the letter is
revealed as that of a 'fictitious testament' like The Testaments
of the Twelve Patriarchs. The present chapter (or 3: 1–16, at
least) is sometimes regarded as an 'Apocalypse of Peter', that
is, a book or tract in which the author prophesies on the
strength of a vision or of a special revelation from a great
figure of the past (perhaps in a dream) what God has determined shall happen in the near future. Sometimes such
writers pretended to be that great figure of the past and so
spoke in his name and with his authority. One of the books
which were to appear later and enjoy some popularity but
finally to be rejected by the church (because not really
by Peter) was actually called an Apocalypse of Peter. The
present passage is hardly an apocalypse. It refers to teaching
given in previous tracts of that kind, and perhaps to the
recorded teaching of Jesus himself. 2 Peter regards 1 Peter as a
recalling of people to what their baptism committed them to.

In the last part of 2 Pet. 2, the author was similarly *recalling* his readers to their Christian way of life. There was a difference in the two situations: 1 Peter is addressed to those who might be tempted to fall away if persecuted, 2 Peter to those who were being tempted to fall away through temptation to lust and similar sins.

2. *Remember the predictions:* see Jude 17, with the note there. Here *God's own prophets* are added to the *apostles* as authorities behind whom stands *the Lord and Saviour* with his final authority. This is very like Eph. 2: 20: 'You are built upon the foundation laid by the apostles and prophets, and Christ Jesus himself is the foundation-stone.' The prophets here are those of the Old Testament. The early church was convinced that all that happened to Jesus which was connected with his ministry and work of redemption was to be found foretold in the scriptures, and the prophets were often mentioned specially, since it was assumed that they had 'prophesied' not simply the will or judgement of God for their own day but events of the distant future. See the explanation on pp. 20f., in the notes on 1 Pet. 1: 10 and 1: 11. *The commands* is a free translation, since the word in Greek is singular. This is well justified because the idea is general: there is no reference to particular *commands* but to the teaching or instruction which Jesus is held to have given through the apostles who are the real authorities appealed to, as in Jude 17.

3–4. *in the last days there will come men who scoff at religion* appears to have been a kind of official warning which takes several forms, though the precise form given to it here and more precisely still in Jude 18 is not known elsewhere, though Jude 18 seems to be quoting some earlier source. Here in verse 4 what the scoffers are going to say need not be taken as an exact prophecy of their words, but rather of the general line they will take. A similar taunt is quoted in 1 Clement 23: 3 f. and 2 Clement 11: 2–4. If we cannot sympathize with their scoffing, we can understand the problem which they raise with the words '*Where now is the promise of his coming?'* Paul had to comfort his converts in Thessalonica, whose *fathers*, too, or some of them, had *been laid to their rest* before the promised coming of the Lord Jesus. 'God will bring them to life with Jesus', Paul assured them (1 Thess. 4: 13–18). That was many years before, and 2 Peter has to answer those who complain that '*everything continues exactly as it has always been since the world began*', reflecting the prophecies of a catastrophic change in the universe which they have not seen fulfilled.

5–7. 2 Peter quite successfully answers the complaint that things have never changed since the creation by drawing attention to two great changes in the historicity of which his opponents would no doubt believe as much as he; this is implied in the reminder that *they lose sight of the fact*, or, as in the N.E.B. footnote, 'They choose to overlook the fact'. He seems to wish to draw attention to one fact only, but incidentally draws attention to the great event of creation itself when the universe was *created by God's word out of water and with water* (Gen. 1: 2, 6, 9). The fact which he has in mind and which he says his opponents overlook is that the *first world was destroyed* —a parallel to what is prophesied has already happened in the Flood (Gen. 7: 21–3 emphasizes very strongly that all life except that in the ark was destroyed by that catastrophe).

The idea that the world was created *out of water* is interesting. The passage must mean that water is the primal material out of which the whole universe was created. Most early philosophers thought the universe was composed of a mixture of basic elements, but Thales of Miletus (dated by his successful prediction of an eclipse of the sun which took place in 585 B.C.) appears to have thought that water was the one basic element out of which everything else was formed. In religious writing only 2 Enoch 47: 4 can be quoted as showing exactly the same belief. The date of 2 Enoch is disputed; the usual view is that it was written about the beginning of the Christian era, but some have argued that it is much later. It is basically Jewish, though certainly hellenistic Jewish, and if written during the

Christian era may have been influenced by Christianity. 2 Peter naturally emphasizes that the creation took place *by God's word*. In verse 7 he repeats that it is *by God's word* that *the present heavens and earth* are *for burning*. Although it was a Stoic belief that the world was due to end in a conflagration and to be succeeded by another age or world, it is not certain that 2 Peter is influenced by Stoicism here, for Zeph. 1: 18 and 3: 8 prophesied the destruction of the earth in the 'fire of the jealousy' of God; cf. Ezek. 36: 5. There is no other passage in the New Testament in which the end of the world is expected to be due to fire; but the idea that it is by fire that *the godless will be destroyed*, which is included in the destruction of the earth by fire here, is to be found in many places in the New Testament; it is based on Mal. 4: 1 which compares the wicked to stubble and prophesies that 'the day that cometh shall burn them up'. Using much the same metaphor, John the Baptist says that the coming One 'will burn the chaff on a fire that can never go out' (Matt. 3: 12). Again, speaking of the final day of the age, Paul says in 1 Cor. 3: 13, 'that day dawns in fire, and the fire will test the worth of each man's work'. How far these expressions are metaphorical is hard to say. This must be the case when Heb. 12: 29 says 'our God is devouring fire', but here in 2 Peter is expectation of a literal destruction of the world by fire. This completes the first argument against the scoffers.

8. The second argument is that God has an entirely different time-scale from man's—*with the Lord one day is like a thousand years*. This is not altogether a good argument. It is a sound statement in itself, but does not really meet the difficulty created by the promises of an early return of Jesus as judge, and as vindicator of his own chosen ones. In 1 Thess. 4: 13–18 Paul has to deal with the problem caused by the fact that some of his converts in the church in Thessalonica have died at all; they evidently had been led by Paul to expect a return of Jesus in their own lifetime. It is only rather later that Paul entertains the possibility that he will die before this

event takes place (he would like 'to depart and be with Christ', he says in Phil. 1: 23); but he does not think of Jesus' return as being much delayed, and we saw that 1 Pet. 4: 13 and 17 (for example) revealed that the author thought that the expected judgement was just starting. The gospels represent Jesus himself as teaching the same most clearly, as for example in Mark 13: 30, where he says, 'I tell you this: the present generation will live to see it all.' It is obvious that here it is the coming of the Son of Man and the attendant events which are referred to. Thus, whatever the true explanation of what Jesus really said, he was reported (and it seems that the church's earliest teachers believed this report) to have taught his followers to expect his early return. However true, therefore, it may be that

> 'A thousand ages in thy sight
> Are like an evening gone',

this does not meet the difficulty which several generations of the church had to face with a sense of bitter disappointment. The thought introduced here is that of Ps. 90: 4, 'a thousand years in thy sight are but as yesterday'. Another passage mentioning a thousand years is Rev. 20: 2 ff., where Satan is to be bound for a thousand years and afterwards released for a short while. These two passages were important for the Christian church, for they introduced a possible solution to the problem of unfulfilled scripture. The solution was taken up by some writers in every generation. It meant that scripture could still be believed as literally true, but it also meant that the hope of speedy deliverance in times of persecution was gone.

9. The third argument is closely connected to the second: *It is not that the Lord is slow . . . but . . . he is very patient with you.* So Paul in Rom. 2: 4 urges that 'God's kindness is meant to lead you to a change of heart'. The thought is developed a little further here into a plan of God to embrace all his creation *because it is not his will for any to be lost, but for all to come to repentance* just as 1 Tim. 2: 4 speaks of God 'whose will

it is that all men should find salvation and come to know the truth'. We saw that in 1 Pet. 3: 19 one interpretation of that passage was that Christ went and preached the gospel to the dead, so that no member of the human race, not even those who had lived before the time of Christ, would fail to hear the gospel. ✳

THE DAY OF THE LORD WILL COME

But the Day of the Lord will come; it will come, un- 10 expected as a thief. On that day the heavens will disappear with a great rushing sound, the elements will disintegrate in flames, and the earth with all that is in it will be laid bare.

Since the whole universe is to break up in this way, 11 think what sort of people you ought to be, what devout and dedicated lives you should live! Look eagerly for the 12 coming of the Day of God and work to hasten it on; that day will set the heavens ablaze until they fall apart, and will melt the elements in flames. But we have his 13 promise, and look forward to new heavens and a new earth, the home of justice.

With this to look forward to, do your utmost to be 14 found at peace with him, unblemished and above reproach in his sight. Bear in mind that our Lord's patience with 15 us is our salvation, as Paul, our friend and brother, said when he wrote to you with his inspired wisdom. And 16 so he does in all his other letters, wherever he speaks of this subject, though they contain some obscure passages, which the ignorant and unstable misinterpret to their own ruin, as they do the other scriptures.

But you, my friends, are forewarned. Take care, then, 17

not to let these unprincipled men seduce you with their
18 errors; do not lose your own safe foothold. But grow in
the grace and in the knowledge of our Lord and Saviour
Jesus Christ. To him be glory now and for all eternity!

✣ 10. That *the Day of the Lord will come...unexpected as a
thief* is the fourth argument, and it consists in reasserting the
great expectation of the early church with confidence. It was
just as much part of the teaching that it would come suddenly
as that it would come early. In 1 Thess. 5: 2 Paul says, 'you
know perfectly well that the Day of the Lord comes like a
thief in the night.' Again, Jesus himself is represented as giving
the same warning, as in, for example, Mark 13: 33–7 which
begins with the words, 'Be alert, be wakeful. You do not
know when the moment comes.'

the heavens were thought of as part of the tangible and
visible universe, not another sphere of existence quite different from ours and in another dimension, as we might imagine.
They are the spheres, containing the sun, moon and stars,
which revolve above the earth and are in the ancient imagination as solid as it. By *the elements* any one of the following
three groups of things may be meant: (1) the four *elements*,
earth, air, fire and water; this sense is common in early Greek
philosophy. In this case fire would be imagined as destined
to destroy fire, but this is not a serious objection to this
interpretation, since the writer may not be thinking very
exactly of this point; (2) the parts of the universe, as pictured
in ancient cosmology, that is, earth, sea, sun, moon and stars.
This would make good sense but the context suggests that the
right interpretation is (3) what are often called the heavenly
bodies, sun, moon and stars by themselves (without earth and
sea). If 2 Peter imagines that these are to *disintegrate in flames*,
it would be natural that *the earth with all that is in it will be
laid bare*, that is, for the coming of the Lord and his inspection.
If we are to read, with some witnesses, as the N.E.B. footnote suggests, not *will be laid bare* but 'will be burnt up',

this meaning for *the elements* (sun, moon and stars) would fit perfectly; the verse would then be a comprehensive prophecy of the destruction of *the heavens* (the spheres containing the heavenly bodies), *the elements* (the heavenly bodies themselves), and finally *the earth with all that is in it.*

11. The interpretation just given makes good sense of the opening words of this verse, which then refer quite logically to *the whole universe*, whose three main parts have just been specified, as due *to break up in this way.*

12. Only here in the whole of the New Testament is there a certain instance of any teaching that men can *work to hasten* ...*on...the Day of God.* The only possible exception to this statement is in Acts 3: 19 where Peter exhorts, 'Repent then and turn to God, so that your sins may be wiped out. Then the Lord may grant you a time of recovery and send you the Messiah...', implying, but not clearly stating, that what men do can have an influence on what God does in the working out of his plan. Apart from that passage and the present passage in 2 Peter, the kingdom or judgement of God is to come entirely from him, and man can do nothing either to hasten or delay it; as we have seen, in the previous passage 2 Peter has been insisting on the suddenness of the expected coming of the Lord and that it is to be expected because it was revealed that it would happen. The way in which the warning of verse 10 is repeated here, that fire *will set the heavens ablaze* and *melt the elements in flames*, once again suggests that *the elements* here means the sun, moon and stars.

13. The *promise* of *new heavens and a new earth* is founded on scripture: Isa. 65: 17 promises, 'For, behold, I create new heavens and a new earth', and an important addition is made in Isa. 66: 22, 'For as the new heavens and the new earth, which I will make, shall remain before me, saith the Lord, so shall your seed and your name remain'—which appears to promise that the Lord's chosen ones will remain undestroyed when he creates the new heavens and the new earth. 2 Enoch 65: 7 f. envisages the end of time, and in rather odd language (the

usual measurements like months and days are to be 'stuck together and not counted'). It prophesies its replacement by the great aeon (or age) which is 'for the righteous' after the great judgement. This is an advance on the Isaiah notions, for here is the idea of an altogether new order to replace the old, not simply a new age to succeed the present age. 2 Peter here follows the ideas of 2 Enoch, in characterizing the *new heavens and a new earth* as *the home of justice. Justice* (or righteousness) is a quality of the whole new creation of God, not merely of the new human race. Probably the writer thought of the new universe as already existing, awaiting the moment when God would bring it into visible being, for the phrase *the home of justice* is, literally in the Greek, 'where justice dwells' (in the present tense).

14. *do your utmost* 2 Peter's practical advice is 'to supplement...faith with virtue' and he has dealt with this in 1: 5–7.

15. In Rom. 2: 4, as already noted in connexion with verse 9 above, Paul teaches that God's *patience with us is our salvation*, and it is noteworthy that 2 Peter adapts this to mean that it is Christ who shows this patience, for we have seen, when discussing Jude 4 and 2 Pet. 2: 1, that in these Letters *our Lord* or 'Master' means Christ and not God the Father.

Paul, our friend and brother, this phrase, in the mouth of one who is representing himself as Peter, betrays a time and sphere in which Peter and Paul are regarded as the chief apostles of the church. This is a view which Acts makes it possible to hold, since in the early part it is Peter who is the chief character in the story (from the beginning to 12: 17, with a brief return in chapter 15), while Paul, who has already captured considerable attention in chapter 9, from 13 onwards commands the stage. 1 Clement 5: 4 f. mentions them together as having similar experiences, and Ignatius, writing to the Romans, when on his way to Rome, to beg them not to prevent his martyrdom, says, 'I do not order you as did Peter and Paul; they were apostles, I am a convict; they were free, I am even until now a slave' (Ign. *Rom.* 4: 3).

These letters belong to the time around the turn of the first to second century, Ignatius' martyrdom being dated perhaps 107. The words *when he wrote to you with his inspired wisdom* have set commentators wondering if the author is thinking of a particular church to whom Paul wrote a letter which he can remember, and to many he appears to have Paul's Letter to the Romans in mind. The opening of 2 Peter is clearly to all gentile Christians in all the churches, and there is little doubt that we have here a situation in which Paul's Letters have become scripture. 2 Peter may therefore be referring to what is usually known as the Pauline corpus (or 'body' of writings), and probably especially to the Letter to the Romans which he regards as addressed to gentile Christians.

16. *in all his other letters* implies that a particular letter is meant in the previous verse, but the word *other* is not in the Greek. Loyal though the author is to the apostles Peter and Paul, he must in honesty admit that Paul's letters *contain some obscure passages.* He might well have been thinking of passages like 2 Cor. 3 or 10: 12–18, for example. It was thus easy for *the ignorant and unstable* to *misinterpret* them *to their own ruin.* We may illustrate this process at work in the matter of the Letters of Paul; it began apparently in Paul's own lifetime. Men perverted his words, not as yet necessarily written ones; for in Rom. 3: 8 Paul refers to this, saying, 'Why not indeed "do evil that good may come", as some libellously report me as saying?' He adds with justifiable indignation, 'To condemn such men as these is surely no injustice.' Perhaps Rom. 6: 1 is another example of things which his opponents claimed had been taught by Paul: he asks, 'Shall we persist in sin, so that there may be all the more grace? No, no!...' The famous passage in Jas. 2: 14–26, which rightly argues, in a way which Paul would have approved, that faith without deeds is useless, may well be directed against people who had mis-understood Paul and misrepresented his teaching by claiming that faith alone could save a man; if this was not *to their own ruin*, it was certainly to that of Paul's doctrine. *The other*

scriptures, if as seems likely the phrase is general and does not refer, as the N.E.B. footnote suggests, to Paul's 'other writings', will embrace many writings indeed. These will be the Old Testament and some books of the intertestamental period, which as we have seen were venerated by both Jude and 2 Peter; it should be noted too that it will embrace much of what we call the New Testament if we are right in thinking that verse 15 implies that Paul's writings had attained the status of scripture.

17. *these unprincipled men* are the 'false teachers' of 2: 1 who combined with their false teaching the following of 'abominable lusts' (2: 10). In 3: 3 f. they are described as 'men who scoff at religion and live self-indulgent lives' and mock at the possibility of the coming of the Lord. Such men might then *seduce you with their errors* because they offer a superficially attractive doctrine of self-indulgence. It seems very likely that it was indeed Paul's doctrine of free pardon by God in Christ and freedom from the Law which lent to them the material which they could pervert. As already explained in the note on Jude 4, these teachers were probably Gnostics of the kind whose main contention was that once a man had attained salvation he could neglect the body and its doings. All that was beneath his notice, and therefore the life of the flesh could be indulged, since it had no effect on the salvation of the soul, which alone was immortal and capable of salvation.

18. What is opposed to these *errors* is the teaching of which 2 Peter has reminded his readers. They are therefore to *grow* not in the intellectual illumination of the Gnostics, who divided their devotees into grades according to their progress in initiation, but in the grace bestowed by God in Christ. He is reminding his readers of what he said in 1: 8, where he urged that gifts such as he has just listed ought to be fostered to prevent Christians from being 'either useless or barren in the knowledge of our Lord Jesus Christ'. As in that passage, there is point in using the technical word of the Gnostics,

knowledge (Greek, *gnosis*). To know Christ is to know him much more in the way a man knows a friend; this is the knowledge required of a Christian, not the intellectual knowledge of these false teachers. This point is made, perhaps, even more clearly if we adopt the translation of the N.E.B. footnote, 'But grow up, by the grace of our Lord and Saviour Jesu Christ, and by knowing him'.

To him are interesting words here, for they manifestly mean Jesus Christ. This makes the final phrase the only doxology (ascription of glory) in the whole New Testament which is certainly to Christ and not to God. Other examples which may be suggested are all uncertain, being probably meant to be ascriptions of glory to God; they are Rom. 9: 5; 1 Pet. 4: 11; Heb. 13: 21 and 2 Tim. 4: 18. This is an interesting indication of the relative lateness of the Letters which can be placed alongside the way in which 'the Lord' means Jesus, and Jesus is regarded as the author of actions which in the scriptures were carried out by God himself. This is fully discussed in connexion with Jude 5 (p. 88). ✻

✻   ✻   ✻   ✻   ✻   ✻   ✻   ✻   ✻   ✻   ✻   ✻   ✻

THE CHRISTIAN HOPE

Reading these three Letters presents us with a problem: it becomes clear that authoritative writers in the church, about the beginning of the second century, eagerly called upon all Christians not only to stand fast in their loyalty to Christ and to the teaching of the apostles, but also to look for a relief from the necessity to 'stick it out' in the shape of the return of Jesus ('the Lord') to judge the world and reward his faithful followers. The hope of this deliverance is presented in 1 Peter as a major source of encouragement to remain steadfast; and when more time has passed than Christians expected, Jude and 2 Peter use both exhortation and warning in insisting that the Lord will come, in spite of the delay. Mixed with the hope, the warning of judgement becomes stronger.

If Christianity is to be presented to modern men, must it include a statement or restatement of this expectation? 2 Peter already betrays the difficulty which it caused: the Lord's return had been promised soon and it had not happened even after the lapse of a generation or more. The author meets this situation with a number of arguments, the most significant of which is that God's time-scale is different from man's. Intending to use a poetic metaphor by comparing a day to a thousand years, he started some people thinking that the Lord would return after a thousand years. In fact in A.D. 1000 there was very widespread expectation of the 'end of the world'. This is a way of restating the Christian hope which was almost accidentally caused and which has no real value for the twentieth century. Even if God's time-scale is indeed different from man's, our difficulty is more radical: we can no longer believe in a literal return of Jesus as Lord, whether 'on the clouds of heaven' or in any other way. The reason for this is not the same as that of the early Christians. It is not that hope has been deferred too long, but that our understanding of the universe precludes the possibility of imagining Jesus, seated on a throne in a literal and geographically identifiable heaven, waiting for the day when he will return to earth. Such ideas belong to mythology and their value is that they express truths which in principle would be expressed otherwise; for example, we might say these ideas mean that Jesus is 'King of men' and by his Spirit seeks to make them all obedient to God.

Much of what used to be called 'the Christian hope', then, dissolves in the 'acids of modernity'. Do there remain any features of permanent value? We have seen that in 2 Pet. 1: 19 the Day of the Lord was envisaged not simply as a day of fateful events in the world but as a day when momentous change would take place in the Christian. Perhaps the root of such hopes is to be found in Paul's expectation of the change of this mortal body into a spiritual body; in 1 Cor. 15: 51 f. he declares 'we shall all be changed in a flash, in the twinkling of an eye, at the last trumpet-call', but in Rom. 8: 11 he thinks of a corresponding gradual transformation which is to lead to this final sudden change: 'God who raised Christ Jesus from the dead will also give new life to your mortal bodies through his indwelling Spirit.' The verse comes at the end of a passage where he insists on the importance of living by the Spirit. In other passages also Paul seems to contemplate a gradual process of 'sanctification' and spiritual advance, as, for example, in Phil. 3: 12 where he says, 'I have not yet reached perfection, but I press on . . .'

The Gospel according to John contributes in a most interesting way to this development of ideas. Here the kingdom of God is treated as a present reality and the whole emphasis falls on the condition of the individual who wishes to be part of it: 'unless a man has been born over again he cannot see the kingdom of God' (John 3: 3). The problem is not 'When will the kingdom come?' but 'How may I enter the kingdom?' Luke 17: 20 f. deals with the same subject rather enigmatically: 'The Pharisees asked him, "When will the kingdom of God come?" He said, "You cannot tell by observation when the kingdom of God comes.

There will be no saying, 'Look, here it is!' or 'there it is!'; for in fact the kingdom of God is among you.''' The Gospel according to John is the most consistent in emphasizing the present reality of the kingdom and of all God's gifts through Christ, but John, no less than Paul and Luke, retains a belief in the last day. According to him, too, he who has faith in the Son will indeed 'possess eternal life' but to this promise is added 'I will raise him up on the last day' (John 6: 40). Throughout the New Testament this expectation persists.

The expectation of a last day, when Jesus the Lord will return, must be abandoned. In practice it has been abandoned; and Christians have laid emphasis rightly, both in practice and teaching, on their present relation to Christ and through him to God, in prayer and sacrament, and by the Holy Spirit. True as this is, it does not follow that we must abandon something which the doctrine of Christ's return implied, and which in essence still holds good. It remains true that 'we must all have our lives laid open before the tribunal of Christ, where each must receive what is due to him for his conduct in the body, good or bad' (2 Cor. 5: 10). No doubt this also is expressed in the language of metaphor; but if we abandon an expectation of a literal coming of the Lord we do not necessarily abandon all that goes with that expectation: we must consider whether behind the metaphorical language there does not lie an indispensable truth. In the case of the actual 'coming' of the Lord we have seen that the essence of it is lost if any attempt is made to allegorize or restate it in any other form. In the case of judgement the matter stands otherwise: God may be regarded as judge of the world in a way or ways unaffected by our giving up expecting the return of the Lord. We may be judged by our compassion or lack of compassion even if there is to be no actual scene, such as Matt. 25: 31–46 depicts for us, of the Son of Man separating the 'sheep' from the 'goats'. How the process of judgement works we cannot know, and our ways of imagining it might be as unsuccessful as those which we abandon;

and the latter remain powerful pictures and symbols, so long as and in proportion as we recognize that they are pictures and symbols and we therefore seek the truth behind them.

In the books of the New Testament printed and discussed in this book we see the gospel applied bravely to a persecution situation, defended fiercely against false teaching and bad example, and compelling some rethinking. This rethinking is nowhere near as profound as that of the Gospel according to John, but these books have the great value of compelling us to think about what is—according to our conviction—of eternal value in the gospel, and how we should apply it to our thinking and our situations. As we do so apply it we must be very certain of one thing: although the early church did expect the Lord's return in a literal way, belief in that hope did not collapse as a result of the continued delay. This shows the extent to which Christians were certain of the redemption already worked in them by the life and resurrection of Jesus, and how to them he was really present in their experience of the Holy Spirit.

A NOTE ABOUT BOOKS

The intertestamental works mentioned in the notes, Jubilees, I Enoch, II Enoch, Testaments of the Twelve Patriarchs, Pirqè 'Aboth (or Sayings of the Fathers) are best consulted in Vol. II of the large *Apocrypha and Pseudepigrapha of the Old Testament* edited by R. H. Charles, O.U.P., 1913, found in most libraries.

For early Christian works such as the letters of Clement and Ignatius see *Early Christian Fathers*, Vol. I of The Library of Christian Classics, S.C.M. Press, 1953, or the Loeb edition of *The Apostolic Fathers*.

✻   ✻   ✻   ✻   ✻   ✻   ✻   ✻   ✻   ✻   ✻   ✻   ✻

INDEX

Abel, 91
Agrippa I, 3
angels, 22, 88 f., 95, 99, 118, 122
apostles as authorities, 97, 101, 129
atonement, 39, 48 f., 61, 117

Balaam, 92, 123 f.
baptism, 15 f., 18, 23, 28 ff., 32, 34, 53 ff., 71, 126

Cain, 91
canon of scripture, 96
Clement of Rome, First Epistle, 5, 120, 129, 136
conscience, 47, 54 f.
covenant, 14 f., 25
creation 130, 134 f.

Dead Sea Scrolls, see Qumran
devil, 56, 70 f., 91, 132
Dionysius, Bishop of Corinth, 5
Domitian, 10

elders, 67 ff.
Enoch, Book of, 51, 89, 95 f., 118
Eucharist, 15, 25, 73, 94, 122
Eusebius, 5, 7, 11 f., 81

Genesis Apocryphon, A, 119
gnostics, 97 f., 112, 118, 138

Hippolytus of Rome, 30, 73
holiness, 24, 26
hope, eschatological, 19 f., 59, 61, 131 f., 140 ff.

Ignatius, 85

James, 81
Jesus Christ
  divine nature, 113
  in Old Testament, 21, 88, 139
  sacrifice of, 14 f., 25 f., 39, 48 f.
  transfiguration, 113 f.
Jubilees, Book of, 51, 96, 119
Jude, 81, 83

judgement, 19, 25, 60, 66, 70 f., 87 ff., 99, 120, 131, 135

kiss of peace, 73

letters in ancient world, 15, 84
Lord's Supper, see Eucharist

Mark, 11, 72
marriage, 34, 41 ff.
Michael, 90
ministry of church, 40, 67 ff.
Moses, 90

Papias, Bishop of Hierapolis, 11
Paul, 29, 34, 45 ff., 58, 62, 85, 87, 109, 125, 130, 136 f.
persecution, 8 ff., 19, 63 ff.
Peter, 3 ff., 7, 10, 69, 100, 106, 111
Pirqè 'Aboth, 124
plan of God, 13 f.
Pliny the Younger, 6, 9
prophets, 20, 32

Qumran, 24, 31 f., 69, 119

resurrection, 18, 26, 50, 56
Revelation, Book of, 10
Roman historians, 34 f.

Satan, see devil
Sayings of the Fathers, see Pirqè 'Aboth
scriptures, church's use of, 20 f., 39, 82, 86, 114 f., 117
Silas, 8, 72
Silvanus, see Silas
slavery, 37 ff.
spirit, 21, 34, 50 f., 60, 98, 117, 141 f.
suffering, 39, 46 f., 58, 61, 64 f.
stars, 95, 115
state, obedience to, 35 ff., 56
Stoicism, 107 f., 131
stone metaphor, 30 ff.

Testaments, fictitious, 12, 86, 111, 128
Trajan, 9 f.